OCR GCSE Home Economics

Child Development

Jean Marshall
Sue Stuart
Revised by Lindsey Robins

Approved publication
OCR
RECOGNISING ACHIEVEMENT

www.heinemann.co.uk

✓ Free online support
✓ Useful weblinks
✓ 24 hour online ordering

01865 888118

Heinemann

Heinemann is an imprint of Pearson Education Limited, a company incorporated in England and Wales, having its registered office at Edinburgh Gate, Harlow, Essex, CM20 2JE. Registered company number: 872828

www.heinemann.co.uk

Heinemann is a registered trademark of Pearson Education Limited

Text © Jean Marshall and Sue Stuart
Revised by Lindsey Robins

First published 2001
This edition first published 2009

13 12 11 10 09
10 9 8 7 6 5 4 3 2 1

British Library Cataloguing in Publication Data
A catalogue record for this book is available from the British Library.

ISBN 978 0 435849 21 4

Edited by Linda Mellor
Designed by Tek-Art
Typeset by Tek-Art
Original illustrations © Pearson Education Limited 2009
Illustrated by Annabel Milne
Cover design by Pearson Education Limited 2009
Picture research by Susie Prescott
Cover photo/illustration © Kimball Hall/Alamy
Printed in Spain by Graficcas Estella

Acknowledgements
The authors would like to thank the following for the use of copyright material: Hackney local authority website screenshot used with kind permission of Hackney Council, p. 11; eatwell plate, Food Standards Agency, Crown Copyright 2007 © Crown copyright material is reproduced with the permission of the Controller of HMSO and Queen's Printer for Scotland, p. 86; One Parent Families/Gingerbread website reproduced with kind permission of One Parent Families/Gingerbread, p. 142.

The authors and publisher would like to thank the following individuals and organisations for permission to reproduce photographs: Alamy/Ianni Dimitrov p. 104; Alamy/Chad Ehlers p. 32; Alamy/Emilio Ereza p. 78; Alamy/Audrey Konovalikov p. 70; Alamy/Adrian Nistor p. 58; Alamy/Chris Rout p. 90; Alamy/Ken Welsh p. 54; Alamy/Blend Images p. 57; Alamy/Bubbles Photo Library pp 34, 50; Alamy/Corbis Super RF p. 87; Alamy/David Hoffman Photo Library p. 136; Alamy/Digital Vision p. 122; Alamy/Itani p. 41; Alamy/JG Photography p. 103; Alamy/Juice Images Ltd pp 43, 104, 124; Alamy/Jupiter Images/BananaStock pp 6, 44; Alamy/Jupiter Images/Goodshot p. 129; Alamy/Jupiter Images/Polka Dot p. 7; Alamy/Mother & Baby Picture Library/Paul Mitchell p. 58; Alamy/Myimagefiles p. 53; Alamy/PBWPIX p. 98; Alamy/Photodisc p. 56; Alamy/PhotosIndia.com LLC p. 58; Alamy/Picture Partners p. 58; Alamy/Radius Images p. 131; Alamy/Redchopsticks.com LLC p. 58; Alamy/Shout p. 39; Alamy/Stockbyte p. 43; Bananastock p. 128; Bananastock/Imagestate p. 88; Blend Images/Getty Images/Ariel Skelley p. 62; Blend Images/Imagestate p. 45; Blend Images/Imagestate/Rolf Bruderer p. 10; Blend Images/Imagestate/Dave and Les Jacobs p. 128; Brand X/Punchstock p. 35; Bubbles Photo Library pp 51, 129; Bubbles Photo Library/Jennie Woodcock p. 118; Corbis Super RF/Punchstock p. 93; Creatas p. 131; Digital Vision/Punchstock pp 62, 122; Dorling Kindersley p. 84; Dorling Kindersley/Vanessa Davies p. 124; Dorling Kindersley/Trish Gant p. 92; Dorling Kindersley/Steve Gorton p.42; Dorling Kindersley/Ruth Jenkinson pp 40, 41, 42; Dorling Kindersley/Dave King p. 124; Dorling Kindersley/Steve Shott p. 130; Getty Images/Altrendo RR p. 6; Getty Images/B2M Productions p. 8; Getty Images/Blend Images/Ariel Skelley p. 40; Getty Images/Photodisc/Keith Brofsky p. 33; Getty Images/Riser/Nicki Pardo p. 6; Getty Images/Stockbyte pp 52, 124, 140; Getty Images/Stone/Ben Edwards p. 38; JGI/Blend Images/Getty Images p. 122; Mother & Baby Picture Library/EMAP p. 54; Moodboard/Punchstock p. 128; Mother & Baby Picture Library/Ian Hooten pp 56, 100, 124; Mother & Baby Picture Library/Ruth Jenkinson pp 38, 56; Pearson Education Ltd/Gareth Boden p. 121; Pearson Education Ltd/Lisa Payne pp 9, 65, 67, 105, 111, 112, 114, 115, 116, 123, 126; Pearson Education Ltd/Jules Selmes pp 51, 55, 56, 57, 58, 117, 146; Pearson Education Ltd/Tudor Photography p. 51; Pearson Education Ltd/Clark Wiseman, Studio 8 pp 90, 95; Photo and Co/Riser/Getty Images p. 70; Photodisc p. 42; Science Photo Library/Neil Bromhall p. 29; Science Photo Library/Veronique Leplat p. 13; Science Photo Library/Dr P Marazzi p. 98; Science Photo Library/Joseph Nettis p. 53; Tudor Photography/Pearson Education Ltd 2005/POD p. 89; Wellcome Photo Library p. 144; Wellcome Photo Library/Anthea Sieveking pp 40, 57, 67, 94, 110, 120, 121, 129.

Every effort has been made to contact copyright holders of material reproduced in this book. Any omissions will be rectified in subsequent printings if notice is given to the publishers.

Websites
There are links to relevant websites in this book. In order to ensure that the links are up to date, that the links work, and that the sites are not inadvertently linked to sites that could be considered offensive, we have made the links available on the Heinemann website at www.heinemann.co.uk/hotlinks. When you access the site, the express code is 9214P.

Contents

This book has been endorsed by OCR to meet the specification requirements for the OCR GCSE in Home Economics (Child Development).

THE SPECIFICATION

The specification seeks to encourage an understanding of the overall needs of young children and the social and environmental influences that affect their development in a contemporary, changing and multicultural society.

Throughout the course you will have the opportunity to:

- increase your knowledge and understanding of human needs, the interdependence of individuals and groups, and the influence of social, cultural and economic factors

- increase your awareness of the implications for Home Economics of rapid technological changes, the use of ICT and the growth of scientific knowledge and understanding, and to develop your ability to respond effectively to such changes

- foster your critical and analytical approach to decision making and problem solving

- develop the knowledge and skills required for the effective and safe management of relevant resources.

You will be assessed in two ways. You will have to do Controlled Assessment (coursework) for up to 60 per cent of the marks. You will also have to do a written examination at the end of the course for up to 40 per cent of the marks.

HOW TO USE THIS BOOK

The book is divided into the following units:

1 Family and parenting

2 Preparation for pregnancy and birth

3 Physical development

4 Nutrition and health

5 Intellectual, social and emotional development

6 Community support

7 Controlled assessment guidance

The first six units cover the content requirements of the specification.

The Controlled Assessment unit gives you some help and guidance on how to tackle your child study task and the short tasks.

Units 1 to 6 cover the topics on double-page spreads, which include the following features.

- Key points – these boxes give you a handy summary of the key learning points throughout a unit.

- Key tasks – questions or exercises to test knowledge and understanding. Questions identified by the 'lightbulb' icon in the Key tasks boxes are designed to extend your understanding of the subject.

- Further work – to give you the opportunity to plan and carry out investigations and tasks, often using ICT.

- For further reference – these boxes provide extra information that you may wish to explore in more depth, often using the Internet.

- Link – these features signpost where content in one unit is linked to content in another unit.

- Think about it – to give you the opportunity to consider your opinions on a particular topic or question.

- Talk about it – to provide the opportunity to discuss particular topics or questions. These can be used in lessons or for revision, and can be done in pairs, small groups or as a class exercise.

- Grade studio – this feature occurs regularly throughout the units. It relates to the written examination in various ways. Practice exam questions may be included or there may be a hint on how to answer a particular question.

- Exam Café – at the end of each of the first six units there are sections to help you revise and prepare for the exam ahead. These pages can be used either for whole-class revision or for individual study. They include useful checklists, ideas for how to revise, examiner tips and a list of key words from the unit.

- Key words are written in **bold** where they appear in a unit for the first time.

HOTLINKS

There are links to relevant websites in this book. In order to ensure that the links are up to date, that the links work, and that the sites are not inadvertently linked to sites that could be considered offensive, we have made the links available on the Heinemann website at www.heinemann.co.uk/hotlinks. When you access the site, the express code is 9214P.

FREE TEACHER SUPPORT MATERIALS

To further support the delivery of this course, a range of activities and PowerPoints have been developed and are available free at:
www.contentextra.com/ocrgcsechilddev
Log-in: ocrgcsechilddev
Password: teacher09

Family structures

A family is a group of people who live together or who are related by marriage or blood. This includes those couples who **cohabit**, which means that they live together without being married. The family forms the basic unit of society in the UK today. It provides for the basic needs of the individuals in the family group. The traditional image of the family unit of two adults and two children is only one of many different types of family structures.

As the UK develops into a wider multicultural society, there is more variety in the type and structure of family units. For example, many families with ethnic origins in Asia have extended family structures that often have three generations living together. These families place great value on the role of the older generation in the structure and functions of family life. Society is more multicultural today, with individuals from differing ethnic and cultural backgrounds marrying and forming new family units.

TYPES OF FAMILIES

The nuclear family

The nuclear family consists of parents and dependent children living together. It is the most common type of family unit. The parents often bring up the children without help from other relations such as grandparents, as they may live a long way from the family. Sometimes parents work outside the home and children are cared for by people who are not related, for example a childminder or staff at a nursery.

A nuclear family

The extended family

The extended family is a nuclear family extended by grandparents or other relations, such as aunts or uncles. The extended family was traditionally a more common family type in the UK, but social changes such as the changing pattern of work opportunities have meant a generation of a family often moves away for work. The extended family has many advantages, such as having more adults in the household to care for the children. In many cultures the extended family is the most common form of family structure, with perhaps three generations of a family living together.

An extended family

The lone-parent family

There are an increasing number of lone-parent families in the UK. Approximately 25 per cent

A lone-parent family

of all families with dependent children are lone-parent families. The lone-parent family has one parent, usually the mother, looking after the child or children. Some lone-parent families were originally nuclear or extended families but the family structure has changed. The lone parent may be unmarried, separated, divorced or widowed.

The reconstituted family

Reconstituted families are families that have changed in structure and re-formed in a new way. These families usually have at least one child who is the natural child of one parent but not both. The family may be made up of children from both parents' previous relationships. In 2000, about one in 12 children were part of a reconstituted family.

A reconstituted family

THE FUNCTIONS OF THE FAMILY

The functions of the family are to provide for the different needs of the family members. These needs vary depending on the individuals who make up the family and the cultural background.

> **The primary functions of the family are to provide for:**
> - the basic physical needs of shelter, food, warmth and clothing
> - protection and support
> - love and security
> - opportunities for learning and development.

SOCIALISATION IN THE FAMILY

Socialisation is another key function of the family. Children need to learn how to live in society, and how to behave and act in different situations – this is called socialisation. The family plays an important role in the socialisation of the child. Being a parent is a very responsible job. Parents often get the blame if their children behave badly or grow up to be antisocial. Although a child's parents may come from different backgrounds and have different ideas about raising children, it is important that they work together, acting as good role models, and guiding and supporting their children.

Families change all the time as individual circumstances change. Roles within families may become more complicated if parents divorce or remarry and traditional roles and individual expectations are also changing. British society is very diverse and ethnic groups differ in their religious beliefs, language, dress style and diet. Expectations for family members differ depending on their cultural background.

The way people think and behave is related to the way they have been brought up. The family gives the child his or her sense of values. Adults are influenced in their approach to parenthood by their own upbringing. Today's children are the future citizens who will, as parents, go on to raise children of their own.

KEY POINTS

- The family forms the basic unit of society.
- The four main types of family structure in the UK are nuclear, extended, lone-parent and reconstituted.
- The family plays a key role in the socialisation of children.
- There are different family structures in other cultures.

KEY TASKS

1 Describe the four main types of family structures in the UK.
2 Explain how the family helps the socialisation of children.
3 Find out and write about two different types of family structures or family patterns in cultures other than your own.

Talk about it

- Does the type of family you are brought up in affect your personality and the way you behave?
- Who influences us the most?

Changing patterns of family life

Families are in a constant state of change as individuals in the family grow older and become more or less dependent on others. The patterns of family life change. Social changes in society, such as attitudes to marriage, affect the pattern of family life. The changes happen to the structure of the family and to the roles and relationships within the family.

> **Reasons for changes to the structure of the family include the following:**
> - changes in the divorce law have made divorce easier for couples. There has been an increase in the number of divorces which, in turn, changes the type of family structures in which children are raised
> - changes in the expectation of lifestyles of men and women affects the age at which people choose to marry, have children and how they split and divide the family responsibilities
> - the availability of methods of contraception allow families to plan when to have children. Families are now smaller than they were 50 years ago
> - changing social and moral attitudes to marriage mean many couples choose to live together and sometimes relationships are less stable. This can lead to an increase in the number of lone-parent families
> - changes in the social welfare system, which offers support to families and can often enable lone-parent families to live independently.

CHANGING ROLES WITHIN THE FAMILY

The roles in the family are changing. Traditionally the father went out to work to provide financially for the family, and the mother stayed at home to look after the children. Changes in society today have meant this happens in fewer family structures. Although the mother still often takes on more of the child-caring responsibilities in the home, the balance of the care is changing.

> **Changes in caring responsibilities can be for different reasons:**
> - when couples marry these days they may have different attitudes and expectations in marriage to those of their parents, and they regard family life as a joint sharing and caring role
> - employment patterns have changed – with many more women working by necessity or choice, this changes the roles within the family
> - in some families the woman may earn more and it is more economically beneficial for the father to be the main carer.

Couples today share family responsibilities

'I feel very privileged being the main carer'

Paul Shaw, 31, is dad to Elliot, three, and Karl, five months. He is married to Simone, 32, a BBC Broadcast assistant. They live in Leigh-on-Sea, Essex.

'I started looking after Elliot a year before Karl was born. Simone had been in her job a long time, whereas I'd only been in mine a year, working in accounts. We were earning about the same, but as I'm quite domesticated, it seemed sensible for me to stay at home.

'Simone found it harder to return to work after Karl was born, but knowing he was with me helped.

'Elliot goes to nursery every day. I feel guilty if I watch TV when Karl has a nap – it's as though I should tidy up instead, to justify being at home.

'My social life is practically non-existent as I haven't been able to keep up with friends but, overall, I feel very privileged being the main carer.

'When Elliot was born I was working six days a week and I didn't feel part of the family. These days my perspective on life is very different and we're happier as a result.'

Shared roles

Most couples starting to have families today see family responsibilities as a shared role. The mother and father do not have separate roles. They may both work and contribute towards the family finances and share the caring and household tasks.

The advantages of families where both parents share the roles are that:

- the family's standard of living will probably improve with both parents or carers working
- fathers have the opportunity to have a closer relationship with their children than in the traditional family role
- children will benefit from a range of caring styles
- children are brought up with the attitude that families share responsibilities, which will, in turn, influence their view of family life when they grow up.

THE INCREASE IN LONE-PARENT FAMILIES

One of the major changes in family structures is the increase in the number of lone-parent families. The rise in the divorce rate is one reason for this increase. The increase in the number of pregnancies outside marriage is another. The changes in social attitudes make it more acceptable today for a child to be brought up in a lone-parent family. Lone parents, like all families with dependent children, come from all ethnic groups.

Family type	Thousands	Percentages
Married couple	8585	66
Cohabiting couple	1412	11
Lone mother	2829	22
Lone father	254	2
All dependent children in families	*13 080*	*100*

Source: ONS

Dependent children in the UK by family type, 2004

The lone parent has to take on the responsibility of two parents. Many lone parents provide happy, stable and caring homes for their children, but some lone parents need additional help and financial support.

KEY POINTS

- Social changes have affected family structures.
- Most couples getting married today see family responsibilities as a shared role.
- The role of women in society is changing and affecting their status in the home.
- There is an increase in the number of lone-parent families.
- Many couples today choose to live together in preference to getting married.

KEY TASKS

1 Explain the reasons for the changes in the structure of the family.
2 How have roles within the family changed over the last 25 years?
3 What are the advantages of sharing the roles within a family?
4 Outline the reasons why lone-parent families are often more dependent on support than other types of family structures.

GradeStudio

Take care when answering questions on changes in the family and family lifestyles. You need to make sure that you do not keep repeating yourself when you describe the changes that have taken place. Learn the facts and stick to them. Marks will be limited if the answer is very repetitive and lacking in information.

Lone mothers are the largest group of lone parents

Children in care

The social services take responsibility for children taken into the care of the local authority. These children are referred to as **children in care**. All agencies which care for children agree that the best place for children is with their families, but there are situations where this is not possible.

> **Sometimes children have to be taken away from their family homes because:**
> - the parent or parents are unable to look after the child because they are ill or in hospital
> - there is evidence of neglect of the child
> - there is evidence of abuse of the child.

If the social services staff feel the child is at risk, they obtain a care order from the court to take the child in to **compulsory care**. Families can ask for their children to be taken into care if they feel they are unable to cope with them.

RESIDENTIAL CARE FOR CHILDREN

Residential homes provide short-term care within a family type of structure. Adult carers take responsibility for small groups of children to build up a secure and caring relationship with them. Children who are taken in to compulsory care have often not experienced the continuity of family life. It is sometimes decided that residential care is the best course of action for some children.

Some children are placed in residential care homes

> **Children are placed in residential homes for many different reasons, for example:**
> - special support and treatment are required, which can best be met by the trained staff in the community unit
> - children in the same family can be kept together
> - the child may have poor experience of **foster care**
> - abuse has occurred within the family, which makes living with another family unsuitable.

Residential care homes play a valuable part in the care system but, wherever possible, children are placed in foster care.

FOSTER CARE

When a child is fostered he or she is placed with another family who will care for and support the child and treat him or her as part of the family. Foster carers need to enjoy looking after children, as many of the children they foster will be emotionally upset and vulnerable. Foster carers do not have any legal rights over a child. They are paid an allowance to cover their expenses in caring for the child. The length of time a child is in foster care will vary according to the individual circumstances of the child.

Foster care can be on a long or short-term basis. Long-term fostering involves the child settling into a pattern of living with the foster family as part of their family. Short-term fostering meets a short-term need and the child is placed temporarily with foster carers; for example when the social services have removed a child from an abusive situation.

The role of foster care

There are more children placed in foster care than in residential care homes as it is thought to be a better type of care for children in care.

> **Foster care is considered to be better because:**
> - it gives the child a family structure and the opportunity to develop relationships with family members
> - it allows the child to develop as an individual
> - foster carers can be more flexible to meet the needs of the individual child than care workers in a residential unit, who have a larger number of children to look after.

Regulation of foster care

Foster carers are checked by the social services department to make sure they are suitable to accept responsibility for children in their care.

> **Foster carers follow guidelines laid down in the Children Act (1989), which include:**
>
> - allowing access to the child's natural parents when it is thought to be in the child's interest
> - bringing up the child in the child's own religion
> - looking after the child with the same care as they would look after their own child
> - returning the child to local authority care when asked.

Local authorities advertise for foster carers

ADOPTION

Adoption is the legal process where adults become parents to children they have not given birth to. The adoptive parents have full legal rights and responsibilities over the child. The adoption process is long and complex. Couples who wish to adopt a child first approach adoption agencies, which can be the local authority or an independent agency. Traditionally couples adopted newly born or very young babies, but social changes in society have reduced the number of babies available for adoption.

> **Social changes include the following:**
>
> - increasing availability of birth control
> - improved support structure for single mothers to keep babies who are born outside marriage
> - society's acceptance of babies born outside marriage.

THE DIFFERENCES BETWEEN FOSTER CARE AND ADOPTION

Both fostering and adoption are alternative ways of forming or extending families, but the responsibility the adults have for the child in their care is different.

A foster parent has:	An adoptive parent has:
• no legal rights over the child	• legal rights over the child
• an allowance to cover the cost of bringing up the child	• to financially cover the cost of bringing up the child
• temporary responsibility for the child.	• permanent responsibility for the child.

KEY POINTS

- Children are taken into local authority care if their parents are unable to look after them, or when there is evidence of neglect or abuse.
- Foster care is seen to be a suitable type of care for children, as it provides a secure family environment.
- There is a reduction in the number of babies available for adoption.

KEY TASKS

1 Explain why children may be taken into the care of the local authority.

2 Suggest reasons why foster care is thought to be the best option for children in care.

3 Describe the differences between adoption and fostering.

4 Why are residential homes only intended to provide care for children on a short-term basis?

Talk about it

The number of babies available for adoption has dropped from approximately 21,000 in 1975 to approximately 4,000 in the year 2000.

In groups discuss:

- why you think that this is the case
- the effects this has had for couples wishing to adopt.

Pre-conceptual health and care

When considering whether to start a family, it is important that both partners are ready to take on the responsibilities of providing for and bringing up a baby and that they both really want a child.

MATURITY

Couples need to be mature enough to cope with parenthood and able to make decisions together over matters such as discipline and education.

Before the baby is born, it can be important to discuss such issues that may arise when bringing up children, as this can help to prepare future parents for the demands ahead of them.

FINANCIAL SUPPORT

In order to maintain an adequate standard of living, finances need to be planned in advance. If both partners work, one partner may decide to leave their job or, if both are to continue working, the cost of child care must be considered. Essential equipment, for example bedding and clothing, have to be provided, as well as the cost of feeding and providing for a growing child.

LINK For more information on preparing for the needs of a baby see pages 40–43.

ACCOMMODATION

A child needs to be provided with a clean, safe environment within a warm and secure home. The accommodation should be suitable for a baby and be adequate to cope with a growing family. There should be somewhere for a baby to sleep and, as the child grows, space to play (e.g. a garden) and a place where the child can keep his or her possessions (e.g. their own bedroom). Facilities that are close by should also be considered, such as parks and pre-school groups.

CHANGING LIFESTYLES

Couples need to consider the roles that each of them will take after the birth of the baby. Parents and carers should be aware that their lifestyles will change considerably once the baby has arrived.

There are many things to consider before having a baby, including finances, accommodation and lifestyle changes

Lifestyle changes can include the following factors:
- one partner may take a career break
- there will be less money available
- there will be a loss of freedom
- babies need 24-hour care
- having a baby means long-lasting responsibilities.

When all the different factors are taken into account and a family is planned for in a thoughtful and caring manner, children can bring a great deal of pleasure, love, satisfaction and new interests for both partners.

CHOOSING WHEN TO HAVE A BABY

With the wide variety of methods of contraception available, couples can choose when to begin a family and how many children they would like. Some couples decide not to start a family until they are older when they are more financially secure. Many women now have very successful careers and are unwilling to lose out on the chance for promotion that they have worked hard for, so they delay having a baby until it is convenient, resulting in higher numbers of older parents.

The advantages of planning a family are that parents are:
- ready to accept the responsibilities of parenthood
- able to space the arrival of each child
- able to provide for each child's physical, social, emotional and intellectual needs
- in a stable, mature relationship.

PRE-CONCEPTUAL CARE

Once a couple has made the decision to have a baby, the woman's health before **conception** must be considered. This is called **pre-conceptual care**.

The main factors in pre-conceptual care are:

- a good, nutritious diet
- not to be overweight
- to be as healthy as possible
- to give up smoking and drinking alcohol
- to avoid taking harmful drugs and medicines
- to check with her GP (doctor) if she is immune to rubella (German measles)
- to have **genetic counselling** if there is concern about hereditary diseases.

Folic acid is found in these foods

Folic acid should be taken by a woman who hopes to become pregnant and during the early months of the pregnancy. It is one of the B vitamins and it helps to prevent defects such as **spina bifida**. This abnormality is caused by the brain and spinal cord failing to develop properly. Good sources of folic acid are nuts, broccoli, wholegrain cereals and wholemeal bread. Folic acid supplements are also recommended and widely available.

Fathers-to-be can support and encourage their partners by also following a healthy diet and giving up smoking, alcohol and drugs. All these factors will help to ensure that the baby will be as healthy as possible.

GENETIC COUNSELLING

Children inherit **genes** from their parents and these genes contain information such as hair and eye colour, body shape, blood group, etc. They may also contain defects or disorders which may result in diseases being inherited by the baby.

Many couples who have a history of a particular disease and who are planning for a baby may require genetic counselling to seek advice on the risk of disease being passed on from parents to children.

Tests can be carried out on the unborn baby to detect any genetic abnormality and, if an abnormality is found, the parents may then be given the option to consider terminating the pregnancy (abortion).

Inherited diseases

Some diseases are caused by faulty genes which can be passed down to generations of the same family.

Examples of inherited diseases include:

- cystic fibrosis – thick mucus blocks the lungs
- haemophilia – where the blood fails to clot
- thalassaemia – a type of anaemia that is a disorder of the red blood cells
- sickle cell anaemia – a disorder affecting the red blood cells
- PKU (phenylketonuria) – the brain becomes damaged causing the child to be mentally handicapped
- muscular dystrophy – weakens the muscles.

KEY POINTS

- **A couple should consider several factors before deciding to start a family.**
- **Contraception allows couples to plan their family and have children when they are ready.**
- **Pre-conceptual care is the health of the woman before conception.**
- **Genetic counselling is beneficial for some couples.**

KEY TASKS

1. Write brief notes on five factors that couples should consider before having a baby.
2. Describe the advantages of planning for a family.
3. Why is pre-conceptual care so important?
4. What do you understand by the term 'genetic counselling'?

Talk about it

- Consider: what is the best age to have a baby?
- Discuss the advantages and disadvantages of having young or old parents.

Family planning (1)

Contraception means 'against conception', in other words in order to prevent having a baby. Family planning means taking action to prevent unwanted babies.

It does not really matter which term you prefer to use: what is important is that all babies that are conceived should be wanted babies.

There is a wide variety of methods of contraception available, so there is lots of choice to meet the needs of different people. Individual needs vary depending on your circumstances, and these change throughout life. It is important to think carefully about what is available and to decide which method is most suited to your needs. Information on contraception can be obtained from a GP or family planning clinic.

There is only one method of contraception which is 100 per cent effective and that can guarantee there are no side effects of any kind, and that is abstention (saying no). The advantage of this is that there is no risk of contracting STIs (see below), including HIV.

Some contraceptives offer protection against **sexually transmitted infections (STIs)** including human immunodeficiency virus (HIV), which is a virus that can be passed from one person to another during sexual intercourse. A person who is HIV-positive may or may not develop a disease called **AIDS**. To prevent passing on these diseases, it is important to use the correct method of contraception. These are known as **barrier methods**.

NATURAL FAMILY PLANNING (NFP)

This involves knowing how to identify the fertile and infertile times of the menstrual cycle. This will show the times when sexual intercourse can take place when it is unlikely that pregnancy will occur. This method is successful only if both partners are committed to the method.

The NFP method relies on the woman using natural indicators:

- temperature – the body temperature rises slightly after **ovulation**. To find out when this happens, the woman's temperature must be taken every morning before getting out of bed and the results recorded on a chart
- cervical secretions – the secretions produced by the cervix change in texture and amount depending on where the woman is in her menstrual cycle.

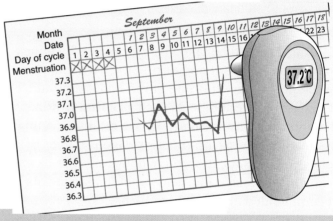

Natural family planning (NFP)

Advantages:

- no chemical agents or physical devices are used
- there are no side effects
- it is acceptable to all faiths and cultures.

Disadvantages:

- it takes between three and six monthly cycles to learn how to use this method effectively, with the guidance of a trained NFP teacher
- daily records must be kept
- intercourse must be avoided during the fertile time
- does not protect against STIs.

METHODS OF CONTRACEPTION

All types of contraception must be correctly used in order to be effective. The type chosen by couples will depend upon their beliefs and requirements. There are many different options available.

Male condom – barrier method: 98 per cent effective if used according to instructions. Condoms are made of thin latex (rubber) and fit over the erect penis. They prevent sperm from entering the woman's vagina. A new condom must be used each time.

Advantages:

- condoms are available free from family planning clinics and sold widely in outlets such as supermarkets and chemists

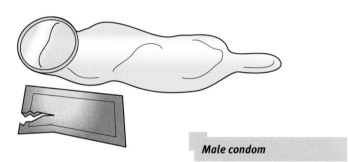

Male condom

- they may protect both partners from STIs, including HIV
- men can take responsibility for contraception.

Disadvantages:

- putting on a condom can interrupt sexual intercourse
- the condom may slip off or split
- the man needs to withdraw as quickly as possible after ejaculation.

Female condom (femidom) – barrier method: 95 per cent effective if used according to instructions. Female condoms are made of soft polyurethane (a type of rubber) and line the vagina and the area just outside. They work by stopping sperm from entering the vagina. A new condom must be used each time.

Advantages:

- female condoms can be inserted at any time before sexual intercourse
- they may protect both partners against STIs, including HIV
- they are sold widely and are available free from some family planning clinics.

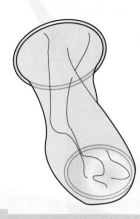

Female condom

Disadvantages:

- putting in the condom can interrupt sexual intercourse
- they are expensive to buy
- you need to make sure the man's penis enters the condom and not between the condom and the vagina.

KEY TASKS

1 Explain how barrier methods of contraception may offer protection against STIs.

2 Describe how the following methods offer protection against pregnancy:

  a the male condom

  b the female condom.

3 What factors affect the success of the natural family planning method?

GradeStudio

Exam tip:

It is important to understand that contraceptives only work if they are used correctly. You need to understand:

- the different types available
- how they are used
- why they work.

Family planning (2)

METHODS OF CONTRACEPTION (CONTINUED)

Combined pill – this is more than 99 per cent effective if used according to instructions. The pill is available from family planning clinics and most GPs. It contains two **hormones**, oestrogen and progestogen, which stop a woman releasing an egg each month (ovulation). Pill users should not smoke.

Advantages:

- it is generally suitable for healthy non-smokers up to the age of the menopause

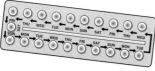

Combined pill

- it protects against cancer of the ovaries, uterus and some pelvic infections

- it often reduces period pain, bleeding and pre-menstrual tension.

Disadvantages:

- it is not suitable for all women

- rare but serious side effects may include blood clots and research suggests an increased risk of cervical and breast cancer

- it is not effective if taken more than 12 hours late or after vomiting or severe diarrhoea

- some medicines may stop the pill from working.

Progestogen-only pill (POP) or mini pill – this is 99 per cent effective if used according to instructions. The POP is available from family planning clinics and most GPs. It contains one hormone, progestogen, which causes changes in the woman's body that make it difficult for sperm to enter the uterus or for the uterus to accept a fertilised egg.

Advantages:

- it is suitable for older women

- it can be used when breastfeeding.

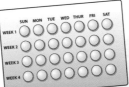

Progestogen-only pill

Disadvantages:

- periods may be irregular

- it is less effective in women weighing more than 70 kg (11 stone)

- it should be taken at the same time each day

- it is not effective if taken over three hours late or after vomiting or severe diarrhoea

- some medicines may stop the pill from working.

Diaphragm (cap) with spermicide – this is 92–96 per cent effective if used according to instructions. Diaphragms must be specially fitted by a GP (doctor) to ensure the right size. They are made of flexible rubber or silicone and are used with spermicide (chemicals that kill sperm). They cover the cervix and must stay in place for at least six hours after intercourse. Fitting must be checked every 12 months.

Advantages:

- there are a variety of different types to choose from

- diaphragms may protect against some STIs and cancer of the cervix

Diaphragm (cap) with spermicide

- they can be put in any time before sexual intercourse.

Disadvantages:

- putting in a diaphragm can interrupt sexual intercourse

- cystitis (bladder infection) can be a problem for some users.

Intrauterine device (IUD) – also known as the coil or loop, this is 98 per cent effective, depending on the type of IUD used. A small plastic and copper device is placed in the uterus by a doctor. It stops sperm meeting an egg or may stop **implantation** of a fertilised egg in the uterus.

Advantages:

- it works as soon as it is inserted

- it can stay in place for three to ten years, depending on the type used

- contraception does not have to be thought about.

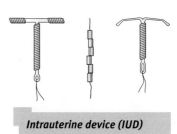

Intrauterine device (IUD)

Disadvantages:

- periods may be heavier and longer
- it is not suitable for women who already have heavy periods
- it is not suitable for women at risk of getting a sexually transmitted disease.

Intrauterine system (IUS) – this is more than 99 per cent effective. A small plastic device is placed in the uterus by a doctor. The device releases the hormone progestogen, which stops sperm meeting the egg and prevents a fertilised egg from implanting in the uterus. Women are taught to check that the IUS is in place by feeling for the threads high in the vagina.

Advantages:

- it prevents pregnancy for five years
- periods will be lighter and shorter
- it works as soon as it is inserted

Intrauterine system (IUS)

- contraception does not have to be thought about.

Disadvantages:

- irregular light bleeding is likely for the first three months
- temporary side effects include breast tenderness and acne.

Contraceptive injection – this is more than 99 per cent effective. The injection releases the hormone progestogen very slowly into the body, preventing a woman from releasing an egg (ovulation). It also thickens cervical mucus to prevent sperm meeting an egg.

Advantages:

- Depo-Provera – the most commonly used contraceptive injection – protects against pregnancy for 12 weeks

Contraceptive injection

- contraception does not have to be thought about
- it may protect against cancer of the uterus and some pelvic inflammatory disease.

Disadvantages:

- periods often become irregular
- regular periods and fertility may take a year or two to return to normal after stopping the injections
- the hormone cannot be removed from the body, so any side effects may continue during the time the injection lasts and some time afterwards
- possible side effects may be weight gain, headaches, acne and tender breasts
- some prescribed medicines may affect the injection.

Implants – these are more than 99 per cent effective. A small, flexible tube is placed under the skin of the upper arm, releasing the hormone progestogen into the bloodstream. The implant stops ovulation and prevents the sperm and egg meeting because of the thickening of the cervical mucus.

Advantages:

- a single tube protects against pregnancy for three years; others work for up to five years
- contraception does not have to be thought about

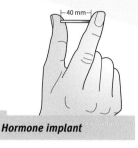
Hormone implant

- once the implant has been removed a woman's fertility returns straight away.

Disadvantages:

- periods are often irregular for the first year
- removal of the implant is sometimes difficult
- possible side effects include headaches, mood changes and weight gain
- some prescribed medicines may affect the implant.

KEY TASKS

1 **Explain how the following methods offer protection against pregnancy:**
   a **The combined pill.**
   b **The progestogen-only pill.**
   c **The diaphragm or cap.**

2 **Describe the differences between an IUD and an IUS and how they work.**

Talk about it

Discuss the factors that are likely to affect the method or type of contraception that individuals choose. How might these choices change at different stages of life?

Family planning (3)

EMERGENCY CONTRACEPTION

If intercourse has taken place without using contraception, or if a method of contraception has failed, it is possible to use emergency methods.

Emergency methods of contraception include:

- Emergency pills (the 'morning after' pill). These must be taken within three days (72 hours) of unprotected sexual intercourse. The pills may delay ovulation or stop a fertilised egg from implanting in the uterus. These pills are mainly provided on prescription by a doctor, although they are now available without prescription in some chemists. It is important to realise that the morning after pill has the effect of starting a period so that the uterus lining is released in order to prevent a fertilised egg implanting. It is not therefore suitable to be used other than in an emergency.

- The copper IUD. This is inserted into the uterus (by a doctor) within five days of having unprotected sexual intercourse. It may stop an egg being fertilised or implanting in the uterus.

PERMANENT STERILISATION

Who can be sterilised?

Both men and women can be sterilised as a method of contraception. Almost any woman can choose to be sterilised and every year thousands of couples choose this as their method of contraception. As of 2005, about 13 per cent of all UK females who are of reproductive age have had the operation. Worldwide, about 150 million women have been sterilised.

It is more usually women over the age of 30 who have already had children who are sterilised; sometimes it is advised for medical reasons. Younger women should think very carefully before agreeing to be sterilised, as the operation is considered to be permanent and is usually irreversible.

Female sterilisation – this is more than 99 per cent effective as a method of contraception. During the operation, the Fallopian tubes are cut, blocked or sealed under general anaesthetic. This prevents the eggs from travelling down the tubes to meet the sperm. Counselling is important to ensure it is the right decision.

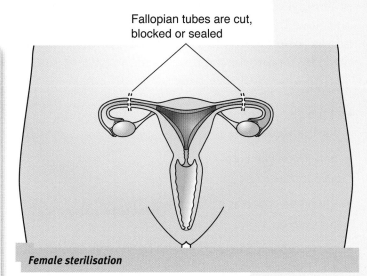

Fallopian tubes are cut, blocked or sealed

Female sterilisation

Advantages:

- it is permanent

- contraception does not need to be thought about if the operation is successful.

Disadvantages:

- the Fallopian tubes may rejoin

- contraception must be used until after the first period after the operation.

Male sterilisation (vasectomy) – this is more than 99 per cent effective as a method of contraception. When men are sterilised, the tubes carrying the sperm (the vas deferens) are cut under a local anaesthetic. This means that sperm are not present in the semen that is ejaculated. Counselling is important to ensure that it is the right decision and that the couple are sure that they do not want children or another child. A vasectomy is a relatively simple, effective method of contraception and is usually considered to be a permanent operation. However, in some cases reversal of the procedure can be attempted, if there is a very good reason to try.

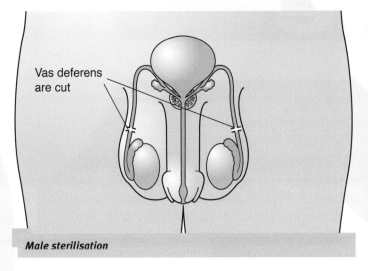

Vas deferens
are cut

Male sterilisation

Advantages:

- it is permanent
- contraception does not need to be thought about if the operation is successful.

Disadvantages:

- contraception must be used until there are two negative semen tests (i.e. no sperm is present)
- it usually takes a few months for no sperm to be present
- the vas deferens may rejoin.

KEY TASKS

1 Describe the emergency methods of contraception available.
2 Why is it important not to rely on the morning after pill as a routine form of contraceptive?
3 Outline the advantages and disadvantages to consider before taking a decision to be sterilised.

Talk about it

Do you think that it should be the male or the female partner who has a sterilisation operation?

FURTHER WORK

Read through the following case scenarios, then using your knowledge of the various methods of contraception available suggest a suitable choice of contraceptive to use in each of the following cases. You need to discuss the alternatives available and offer practical advice, giving reasons for your suggestions.

- Shelley is 17 years old and has just started going out with Kevin; she is considering having sex with him. How would you advise her?
- Kirsti and Rhuari have been married for 20 years and have three teenage sons. Kirsti is sure that she does not want any more children but Rhuari is only just starting to think the same way. What should they do?

- Joel and Usha are to be married in a few weeks' time. They have occasionally had unprotected sex and are wondering what, if anything, they should do about using a contraceptive. What do you think?
- Maryam has reached the menopause. She and David do not have sex as often as they used to, but a baby right now would be a disaster for them both. David cannot be bothered to think about contraception – he thinks that's a woman's job! What should Maryam do?
- Jade and Lenny have four children under the age of five years. So far they have tried the NFP method, but it has not been very successful. They cannot afford or cope with any more children, but they are both only 25 years old. What do they need to do?

ExamCafé

Welcome

These sections in the book have been included to help you think about what you have learned so far, and to revise for your written exam. Exam Café pages are designed to be used by students and are suitable for individual revision sessions or group or class revision sessions, as required.

It is time now to review what you have covered in this unit. Exam Café will help you remember the main information that you have learned in each section and will give you useful hints, revision tips and some sample questions and answers. These will really help you revise, so relax, make yourself a cup of tea or coffee, and get started!

No one except you really knows just what it is that helps you remember what you have learned. Was it that really good lesson that Nurse Wendy came in for – or was it the silly antics of your teacher one day?

Different things help different people remember what they have learned. You will probably have done lots of sessions on 'how we learn best', but what really matters is that you know what you need to know, by the day of your exam. The important point to remember is – don't panic! Revise what you have learned and you will be just fine.

Revise little and often. Work out a plan that suits you and stick to it. So, here goes… with some hot tips from people who know how you feel right now...

> When revising I often work with my friend Katy to create notes to read over and over. That helps me a lot, as I like the company. Then we ask each other questions, like: 'What are the advantages and disadvantages of:
> * A nuclear family
> * An extended family
> * A step family?'
>
> **Dannique**

Revision

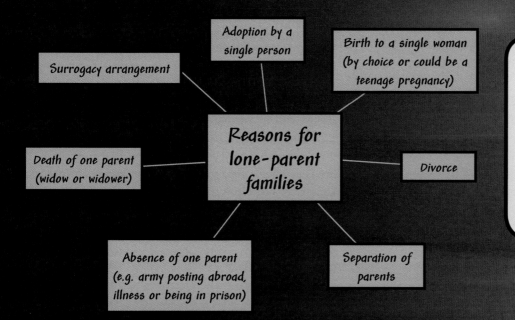

Surrogacy arrangement

Adoption by a single person

Birth to a single woman (by choice or could be a teenage pregnancy)

Death of one parent (widow or widower)

Reasons for lone-parent families

Divorce

Absence of one parent (e.g. army posting abroad, illness or being in prison)

Separation of parents

> I find mind maps and spider diagrams useful as they produce visual images which make information easier to remember. They help me to organise my thoughts and connect different sections of topics together.
>
> **Annie**

Revision checklist

Things I really need to remember…

Unit 1 revision checklist: family and parenting		
Family structures	• 4 main types of family – nuclear, extended, lone-parent, reconstituted	❏
	• Fostering and adoption	❏
Changing patterns of family life	• Changing role of women in society	❏
	• Family responsibilities shared between the couple	❏
	• Increase in lone-parent families	❏
	• Changing roles in a diverse society	❏
Children in care	• Reasons why children are taken into care	❏
	• Reduction in number of children available for adoption	❏
	• Foster care provides secure family environment	❏
Pre-conceptual health and care	• Factors to consider before starting a family	❏
	• Advantages of planning a family	❏
	• Genetic counselling	❏
	• Pre-conceptual care of the mother	❏
Family planning	• Contraception methods	❏
	• Sterilisation	❏
	• Emergency contraception	❏

Common mistake!

An error made by lots of people is to confuse the terms **conception** and **contraception**.

Conception means the joining of an egg and a sperm.

Contraception means to prevent having a baby.

I find it useful to make a checklist to help me remember, a bit like the one I have started here. I read through my classwork and then put the information into a table which I use to go over time and time again to learn the facts. Try it for yourself… see what you think!

Amelia

Methods of contraception checklist		
Method	Advantages	Disadvantages
Male condom	• Available free from family planning clinics • Protects against the spread of STIs • Can buy from many places	• Putting it on can be inconvenient • It may split • It must be used correctly
Contraceptive pill	More than 99% effective if taken at the same time daily	• You need medical advice to get it • Not reliable if taken late or if you have sickness
Natural family planning		
Diaphragm with spermicide		

ExamCafé

Exam preparation

Unit 1 sample exam question

Tips
The number of marks the question is worth will always be shown at the end of the question in brackets.

Why is pre-conceptual care important? **(8 marks)**

Student answer

The mother-to-be's health is important to try to ensure a healthy baby. Pre-conceptual care takes place BEFORE planned conception so she should have a healthy diet, containing a wide variety of nutrients, including protein, iron and calcium. It should be especially rich in folic acid to prevent spina bifida. Alcohol should be avoided and so should drugs, including medicines from the GP. She should not be overweight and exercise should be taken regularly. Her immunity to rubella (German measles) should be checked as it can be very harmful to the unborn baby during the first few months of the pregnancy. If she smokes she should definitely stop as there is lots of proof that smoking causes smaller babies and can result in a miscarriage. The mum needs to be as well as possible before she conceives.

Examiner says:
There is a good level of explanation here and it includes enough detail for 5 marks.

Examiner says:
The student realises that a healthy diet is needed but she does not say what the nutrients are needed for, although she does include the importance of folic acid. Ensuring that all three of the points about drugs, alcohol and smoking are included is essential in an answer of this type. The answer clearly shows that she realises that pre-conceptual care is before the baby is conceived and that immunity to rubella is important. She is aware of the value of exercise. To improve this answer she could have explained why the answers she gave are important to a woman's pre-conceptual health.

Practice questions

1 There has been an increase in the number of lone-parent families.
  a Explain the term 'lone-parent family'. **(1 mark)**
  b Suggest reasons for the increase in the number of lone-parent families. **(2 marks)**
  c Identify the benefits that are available to support the lone-parent family. **(5 marks)**

2 Family structures in our multicultural society are changing.
  a Describe the structure of the:
    i nuclear family
    ii extended family
    iii reconstituted family. **(6 marks)**
  b Explain the reasons why family structures are changing. **(8 marks)**

3 a Name the organisation responsible for arranging foster care. **(1 mark)**
  _____

  b Identify three features of foster care. **(3 marks)**
    1 _____
    2 _____
    3 _____

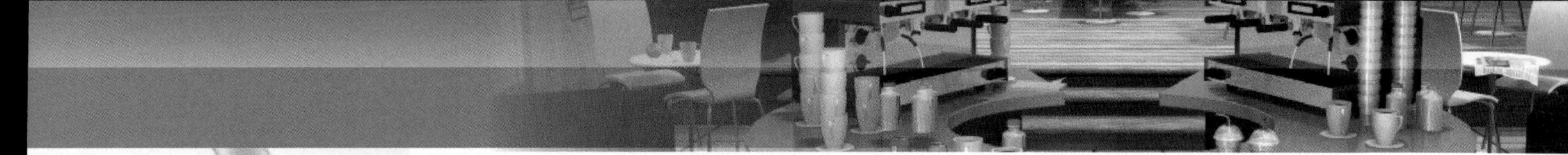

4 a Women have a choice of contraceptives available to them. Identify the following methods of contraception.

Description	Method of contraception
A rubber cover placed over the cervix	
A device placed in the uterus by a doctor	
Taken orally and contains hormones	

(3 marks)

b List two methods of contraception that do not require medical advice.

1 ______________________________

2 ______________________________

(2 marks)

The following answers would be accepted:
CAP/diaphragm
IUD/IUS/IUCD/coil/copper T/copper 7
The pill/combined pill/mini pill

Two of these would have been an acceptable answer:
- femidom/female condom
- condom
- rhythm method/natural family planning
- abstention or saying no

Key words	
AIDS	Acquired Immune Deficiency Syndrome, caused by the HIV virus
barrier methods	contraceptives that protect against sexually transmitted infections
cohabit	to live together without being married
compulsory care	taking a child who is at risk into the care of the local authority
conception	the joining of an egg and a sperm
foster care	when a child is looked after on a temporary basis by adults other than his or her own parents
genes	found in all living cells and contain information, such as hair and eye colour
genetic counselling	consulting an expert on hereditary diseases
hormones	chemical messengers that travel through the bloodstream
implantation	when the fertilised egg becomes attached to the uterus lining
children in care	children who have been taken into the care of the local authority
ovulation	when an egg is released from the ovary
pre-conceptual care	the health of the expectant mother before conception
spina bifida	an birth defect whereby the spinal cord fails to develop properly
STIs	sexually transmitted infections

Reproduction

When a couple have sexual intercourse, the sperm from the man may fertilise an egg from the woman and a baby will be conceived. In order to understand this process, it is important to know about the female and male reproductive systems.

THE MALE REPRODUCTIVE SYSTEM

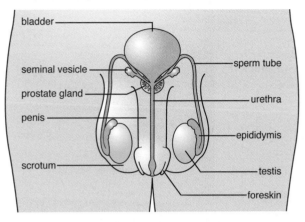

THE FEMALE REPRODUCTIVE SYSTEM

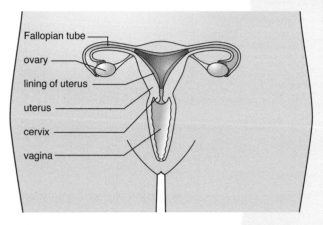

Seminal vesicle – stores and secretes semen, which carries the sperm

Scrotum – the bag containing the testes

Testis – produces sperm and the male sex hormone

Sperm tube – lead from the testes, and along which the sperm travel

Urethra – a tube which carries semen and urine

Penis – becomes erect before and during intercourse and ejaculates sperm into the vagina

Foreskin – covers and protects the tip of the penis

Epididymis – where the sperm are stored

Fallopian tube – joins the ovaries to the uterus. Fertilisation takes place here

Ovaries – control the female sex hormones and produce and release eggs

Uterus – where the baby develops and grows

Lining of the uterus – every month during menstruation, this comes away. If an egg is fertilised, it becomes attached to the lining

Cervix – the neck of the uterus that is usually closed

Vagina – during intercourse, sperm are deposited here

MENSTRUATION

The average menstrual cycle takes 28 days to complete. The purpose of the cycle is to produce an egg and to prepare the uterus to receive the egg if it is fertilised.

During the first part of the cycle, the lining of the uterus is built up ready to receive an egg. If the egg is not fertilised, the lining of the uterus breaks down and leaves the body in a flow of blood called **menstruation** or period.

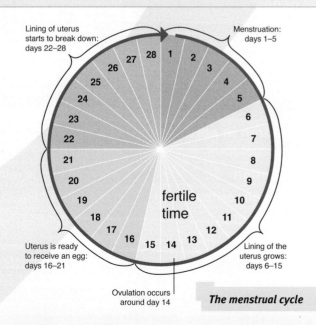

The menstrual cycle

Usually an egg is released every month alternately from one of the ovaries. It is released about halfway through the menstrual cycle on around day 14. This process is called ovulation. After the egg is released from the ovary, it moves along the Fallopian tube.

FERTILISATION

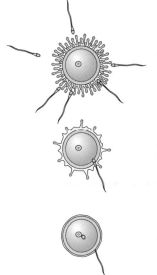

Sperm meets the egg in the Fallopian tube

One sperm penetrates the egg's outer membrane

The sperm joins the egg – the sperm's tail is left behind

The fertilised egg travels down the Fallopian tube to the uterus and divides into cells

How fertilisation takes place

Before intercourse, a man's penis becomes erect and it is then able to enter the woman's vagina and ejaculate semen. Semen is a milky substance that contains millions of sperm. From the vagina, the sperm swim into the uterus and along the Fallopian tubes. If an egg has been released from an ovary (ovulation), the sperm may meet an egg in the Fallopian tube. If this occurs, the egg will be fertilised by one of the sperm. Conception will have taken place. A fertilised egg contains 46 chromosomes or 23 pairs of chromosomes.

The fertilised egg travels down to the uterus. It divides into cells that become attached to the uterus lining, where it will develop and grow into a baby. This is called implantation.

HORMONES

Hormones play an important part in controlling the menstrual cycle. They act as chemical messengers, travelling through the bloodstream and carrying messages to different parts of the body. The hormones from the pituitary gland stimulate the ovaries and the testes to produce the sex hormones. The female sex hormones (oestrogen and progesterone) are produced by the ovaries. The male sex hormone (testosterone) is produced by the testes.

 KEY POINTS

- **Menstruation occurs on average every 28 days.**
- **Ovulation has occurred when an egg has been released from the ovary.**
- **Fertilisation is when an egg and a sperm join together in the Fallopian tube.**
- **Implantation is when the fertilised egg becomes attached to the uterus lining.**

KEY TASKS

1 **Describe the functions of the following:**
  a **Fallopian tube.**
  b **Ovaries.**
  c **Uterus.**
  d **Seminal vesicle.**
  e **Testes.**
  f **Sperm tube.**
2 **Study the diagram of the menstrual cycle.**
  a **For how many days does menstruation take place?**
  b **On what day is ovulation likely to take place?**
  c **After ovulation, what is the uterus ready to receive?**
  d **How many days, on average, does the menstrual cycle take to complete?**
3 **Explain the following terms:**
  a **Ovulation.**
  b **Fertilisation.**
  c **Implantation.**
4 **Where in the female reproduction system does fertilisation usually take place?**
5 **Describe the factors that can cause variations in the menstrual cycle.**

 GradeStudio

In the exam it is unlikely that you would be asked to draw diagrams like those shown here. But it is a good tip to learn the labels of the male and female reproductive systems thoroughly and to make sure that you are really clear about how fertilisation takes place. You will then be able to label any diagrams in an exam question and describe the process if needed.

The development of the embryo and foetus

Once the fertilised egg is implanted into the uterus lining, it is called the embryo. The time between conception and birth is called pregnancy and lasts, on average, for 40 weeks from the first day of the last menstrual period.

DEVELOPMENT

The cells develop very rapidly once implantation has occurred, and these become the embryo. The embryo develops blood, bone and muscles, and the heart starts beating at around three weeks after conception. The embryo is barely 3 mm long

After eight weeks, the embryo is called the foetus. All the main organs of the body are developing and the limbs, hands and feet are forming. The foetus is now 4 cm long

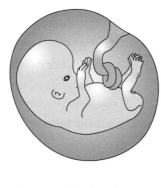

At around 20 weeks, the heartbeat can be heard and the foetus is about 25 cm long and weighs around 350–400 g (12–14 oz)

At 28 weeks the foetus is very energetic and kicks freely. The skin is covered in fine, downy hair called lanugo and a greasy coating called vernix. The foetus is about 38 cm long and weighs around 900 g (32 oz)

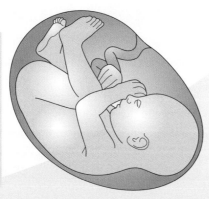

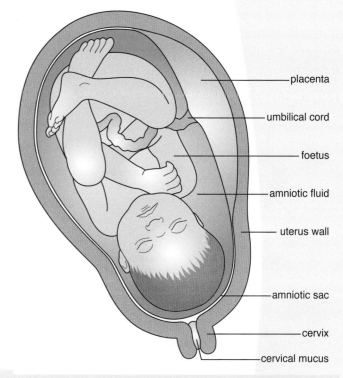

- placenta
- umbilical cord
- foetus
- amniotic fluid
- uterus wall
- amniotic sac
- cervix
- cervical mucus

At around 40 weeks the foetus is ready to be born. The lanugo will usually have disappeared, but the vernix will remain covering the skin – it is reabsorbed after the birth. The average weight of a baby at birth is approximately 3–3.5 kg (7–7.5 lb) and average length is 50–55 cm

SUPPORT AND NOURISHMENT FOR THE FOETUS

The fertilised egg not only produces the embryo, it also provides the foetus with the placenta, the **umbilical cord** and the **amniotic sac** which provide nourishment and support until birth.

The placenta

The placenta is an organ that is made of soft spongy tissue. It is attached to the wall of the uterus. It is fully formed by the twelfth week and grows steadily to keep pace with the developing foetus.

The main functions of the placenta are to:
- provide the foetus with nutrients
- provide oxygen to the foetus
- remove carbon dioxide produced by the foetus
- excrete waste material.

Harmful substances such as alcohol, nicotine, viruses and medicines can cross the placenta from the blood of the mother to the blood of the foetus. These may damage the developing foetus, especially in the first three to four months of pregnancy.

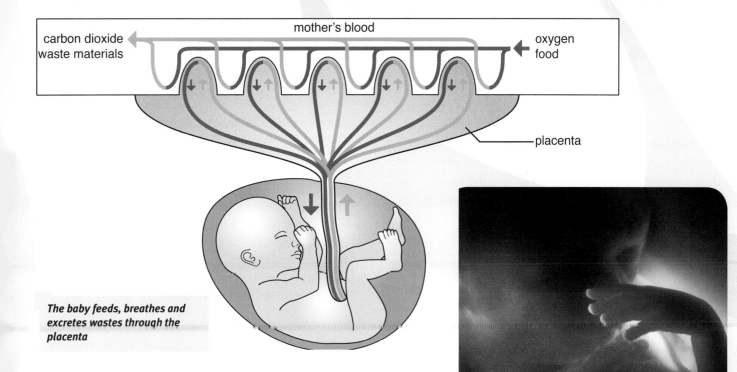

carbon dioxide waste materials

mother's blood

oxygen food

placenta

The baby feeds, breathes and excretes wastes through the placenta

A foetus at about 18 weeks

The umbilical cord

The placenta is linked to the foetus by the umbilical cord, which will grow to be about 50 cm long. The cord contains blood vessels that carry blood to and from the placenta to the foetus.

The amniotic sac or amnion

The foetus develops inside the amniotic sac, which is filled with amniotic fluid. The fluid protects the foetus from being damaged and cushions it from any shocks.

MISCARRIAGE

Sometimes, problems can occur in pregnancy and a woman may experience a miscarriage – the accidental ending of a pregnancy. Miscarriages most often occur in the twelfth to the fourteenth week and are often the result of the baby or the placenta not developing properly. Subsequent miscarriages may be avoided if the reason for the first can be identified.

ECTOPIC PREGNANCY

An ectopic pregnancy occurs when the fertilised egg implants itself outside the uterus. The most common place for this to happen is in the Fallopian tube. Fallopian tubes have cilia (tiny hairs) that move in waves to encourage the egg towards the uterus. If these cilia are damaged or the tube is blocked, ectopic pregnancy is more likely. Ectopic pregnancy is fairly rare but it can be very dangerous for the mother.

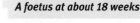 **KEY POINTS**

- Lanugo is fine, downy hair on the foetus's skin.
- Vernix is a greasy coating covering the skin.
- After eight weeks, the embryo becomes the foetus.
- Pregnancy lasts for approximately 40 weeks.
- The placenta, umbilical cord and amniotic sac are the support structures for the foetus.

KEY TASKS

1 Describe briefly how the embryo and foetus develop up until birth.

2 What are the functions of the placenta?

3 Explain the following terms:

  a Vernix.   c Amniotic sac.

  b Umbilical cord.   d Lanugo.

4 Explain the meaning of the term miscarriage and suggest some possible causes.

Infertility

The term infertility means being unable to conceive and affects up to one in six couples. There are several reasons for infertility and advice can be obtained from a GP (doctor), a family planning clinic, a specialist charity or an infertility clinic. Some couples will need advice and reassurance; others may need drug therapy or surgery.

CAUSES OF INFERTILITY

If a couple have been trying for a baby for at least two years without success, there are many tests that can be carried out to help discover the reasons why.

Possible reasons for infertility include:

- a low sperm count – this is when there is a low number of sperm in the semen. A high number of sperm need to be ejaculated at any one time to ensure that conception takes place. Medical conditions, e.g. mumps in boys aged 12 years and over, can cause the sperm count to drop dramatically
- failure to ovulate – this is when the ovaries do not produce eggs. This could be due to hormonal problems or to taking the contraceptive pill for a long time (it often takes time for the menstrual cycle to return to normal, although this is usually only a temporary problem)
- blocked Fallopian tubes – the Fallopian tubes could be blocked, perhaps by an infection, and conception cannot take place
- the cervical mucus in the neck of the uterus may be too thick, preventing the sperm from entering
- the man or woman might have had treatment for cancer, leaving them infertile.

Once tests have established the reason why a couple may be experiencing problems conceiving a baby, advice can be given about any possible treatments. Even after tests, the cause of the infertility may remain unexplained and in vitro fertilisation (IVF) treatment may be suggested to bring the sperm and the eggs together outside the body.

POSSIBLE TREATMENTS

There are a number of possible treatments available, depending on the reason for the infertility.

Possible treatment	Reason for infertility
Drug therapy	To control ovulation if a female is not producing eggs for hormonal reasons. The drugs stimulate egg production and ovulation. This method can cause several eggs to be released together and can result in multiple births, e.g. twins or triplets.
Surgery	To improve or repair blocked or damaged Fallopian tubes.
Artificial insemination	Using the partner's sperm, or sperm from someone else if the partner has a low sperm count. Artificial insemination involves the injection of sperm into the uterus at the time of ovulation and then fertilisation may take place in the usual way. This may be suitable for women whose cervical mucus is too thick for sperm to enter the uterus.
In vitro fertilisation (IVF)	The woman's egg is removed from the ovary and fertilised with the man's sperm in a laboratory. When the **embryo** is a few days old, it is placed in the woman's uterus and may then develop in the usual way. In order to improve the success of this method, several eggs are fertilised at the same time and returned to the woman's uterus, so this method can result in a multiple birth. This technique is suitable for women with blocked or damaged Fallopian tubes.
Egg donation with IVF	If a woman cannot produce eggs of her own, another woman donates an egg to be fertilised by the first woman's partner.

Embryo donation	The egg of a woman and the sperm of a man are fertilised using IVF and placed in another woman's uterus. This method could be suitable for those couples who cannot produce eggs and who have a low sperm count.
Gamete intra-Fallopian transfer (GIFT)	Using the couple's own or donated eggs or sperm, GIFT is a method where the eggs and sperm are removed and placed in the Fallopian tubes to be fertilised. This technique may result in a multiple birth and it is suitable for couples who cannot produce eggs and have a low sperm count, or who cannot conceive in the normal way.
Intra-cytoplasmic sperm injection (ICSI)	This is a technique where a single sperm is injected into an egg in a laboratory. Two embryos may be produced, which are then transferred to the uterus in the same way as with IVF. This method is appropriate when the sperm count is low.

MULTIPLE BIRTHS

Multiple births can, and do, happen naturally, but some fertility treatments may result in births where there is more than one **foetus** developing in the uterus.

A multiple birth occurs when:

- one fertilised egg splits into two parts and develops into two separate individuals, producing identical twins. If the split is incomplete, this results in the twins remaining joined together; they are called conjoined or Siamese twins
- two or more eggs are fertilised by different sperm, producing non-identical twins, triplets, quads, quins or sextuplets.

Identical twins

Identical or uniovular twins share the same **placenta** inside the uterus as they grow and develop. These twins are the same sex and are alike in appearance as they have inherited identical genes.

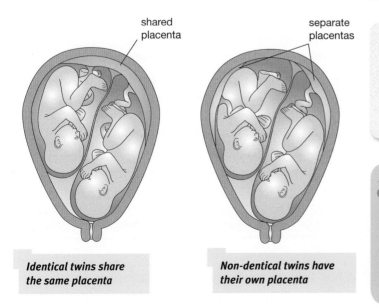

shared placenta

separate placentas

Identical twins share the same placenta

Non-dentical twins have their own placenta

Non-identical twins

Binovular or fraternal twins develop when two eggs are released at the same time and are both fertilised by different sperm. They have separate placentas.

Non-identical twins can be the same sex, or a boy and a girl. They are no more alike than any other children of the same family.

KEY POINTS

- **There are many different causes of infertility.**
- **There is a wide variety of possible treatments.**

KEY TASKS

1 **Define 'infertile' and list the main causes of infertility.**
2 **Describe how artificial insemination may result in an egg being fertilised.**
3 **How do non-identical twins differ from identical ones?**
4 **Explain the following terms:**
   a IVF.   b GIFT.   c ICSI.

Talk about it

- Discuss the possible complications that may arise with multiple pregnancies. Could you cope?
- Do you think it is right to separate conjoined twins, even if the operation is life-threatening?

GradeStudio

When answering exam questions relating to twins remember that the examiner may use any of the different names for twins – so be sure to learn all of the terms. Do not muddle up the names or you may lose valuable marks.

Health and well-being in pregnancy

SIGNS OF PREGNANCY

The first sign of pregnancy that a woman may experience is a missed period. Other signs of pregnancy may include:

- nausea (known as 'morning sickness' as it often occurs first thing in the morning)
- tender and enlarged breasts
- passing urine more frequently
- darkening of the skin around the nipples
- constipation.

HEALTH FACTORS TO BE CONSIDERED

The woman needs to consider several factors during the pregnancy to ensure that both she and the unborn baby are as healthy as possible.

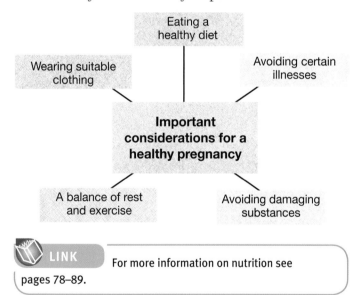

 LINK   For more information on nutrition see pages 78–89.

EATING A HEALTHY DIET

During pregnancy, it is important to eat a variety of foods to ensure a well-balanced and nutritious diet.

A healthy diet should include:

- foods rich in protein, e.g. lean meat, chicken, eggs, pulses (such as lentils or beans) and fish, especially oily fish
- starchy foods, including bread, potatoes, pasta and rice (if possible these should be wholegrain options as they contain more nutrients and fibre)
- dairy foods, such as cheese, yoghurt and milk, which are all rich in calcium
- at least five portions of fruit and/or vegetables a day plus a glass of fruit juice
- iron-rich foods to prevent anaemia, e.g. green leafy vegetables
- only small amounts of fatty and sugary foods to prevent excessive weight gain.

Folic acid is extremely important, especially in early pregnancy, as it reduces the risk of the baby developing a neural tube defect, such as spina bifida.

Breastfeeding

If the mother is going to breastfeed her baby, her diet should be similar to when she was pregnant. Eating sensibly is very important in order to stay healthy. Very often, the mother may eat more when breastfeeding, or lactating, and it is advised that she increase her intake of starchy foods. She should also maintain a good intake of calcium by drinking a pint of milk and eating some cheese and yoghurt every day. Alcohol intake should be kept to a minimum.

LINK   For more information on lactation see pages 78–79.

AVOIDING CERTAIN DISEASES

Listeriosis is a rare disease caused by bacteria which grow in certain foods. An attack of this disease can result in miscarriage, stillbirth or illness in the unborn baby.

A pregnant woman should avoid eating:

- soft cheeses, e.g. Brie and blue-veined cheese
- cook-chill meals unless they are very hot all the way through
- meat or fish which is not cooked thoroughly
- products containing raw eggs (e.g. mayonnaise) which may contain salmonella bacteria
- liver and foods containing liver (such as paté) should be avoided as liver contains large amounts of vitamin A which could harm the unborn baby.

A few infectious illnesses can cause serious problems if contracted and should be avoided.

A pregnant woman should avoid any contact with these diseases:

- Rubella (German measles) – if rubella is caught in early pregnancy (before 16 weeks), although the mother may be unaffected it can cause severe abnormalities in the unborn baby, including deafness, blindness, heart disease and brain damage.

- Toxoplasmosis – this disease can be passed on by contact with cat faeces, therefore pregnant women are advised not to touch cat litter trays. The disease is usually unnoticed in the mother, but if passed on to the unborn baby it may cause serious problems.

- Chickenpox – pregnant women are advised to avoid children with chickenpox and adults with shingles. If contracted during pregnancy, the mother may become ill and the unborn baby may be affected.

AVOIDING DAMAGING SUBSTANCES

There are some substances that can cause deformity in the developing baby and should be avoided by the expectant mother, as outlined in the table below.

Substance	Possible effects
Medicines	Many medicines are harmful to the unborn baby and should only be taken under the advice of a doctor.
Illegal drugs such as LSD, crack, cannabis and heroin	These drugs affect the mind and are habit-forming and the baby may be born addicted to the drug.
Alcohol	Recent research suggests that alcohol should be completely avoided during pregnancy if possible. Regular drinking can interfere with the baby's development, causing foetal alcohol syndrome.
Smoking	Smoking can seriously damage the health of both the mother and the unborn baby. The baby is more likely to have a low birth weight and poor lung function, and to be more vulnerable to illness and cot death.
Aromatherapy/ essential oils	These may cause miscarriage.

A BALANCE OF REST AND EXERCISE

Regular exercise is recommended for everyone, including the expectant mother. It will ensure that she keeps in good health and helps to prevent excessive weight gain. Activities such as swimming, walking and cycling are particularly beneficial providing they are done in moderation. Exercise should be balanced with rest and towards the end of pregnancy a rest during the day will also be beneficial.

WEARING SUITABLE CLOTHING

During pregnancy, the expectant mother's breasts enlarge and the abdomen expands. Therefore, clothing needs to be loose and expandable in order to be comfortable. Well-fitting, supportive bras are important, as well as comfortable shoes with low heels. Suitable footwear will help the mother's balance and prevent backache.

KEY POINTS

- A healthy lifestyle for the expectant mother is vital to ensure her unborn baby is as healthy as possible. She should not smoke and should avoid alcohol.
- Eating a balanced diet and avoiding particular diseases should help her maintain a healthy lifestyle.

KEY TASKS

1 Describe the type of diet an expectant mother should follow.

2 Explain the diseases that should be avoided by an expectant mother.

3 What effects does smoking have on the unborn baby?

4 Design an advice sheet to be given to pregnant women which outlines the key things they need to be aware of during pregnancy.

FURTHER WORK

Plan and prepare a healthy lunch-time meal for a pregnant woman. Explain which nutrients are provided by the meal, and how it fits in with her dietary needs.

GradeStudio

Remember: a question referring to alcohol and/or smoking will always expect you to understand that they can cause *serious* problems to the unborn child.

Antenatal provision (1)

ANTENATAL CARE

Antenatal ('before birth') care is provided during pregnancy and involves regular check-ups and tests. These are carried out to ensure that the baby is developing normally and that the pregnancy is going well. The first antenatal check-up takes place within the first 12 weeks of pregnancy and checks are then carried out every month until week 30, when more frequent checks are required.

Attending antenatal appointments is very important and the father may also attend to answer questions about his family history and have blood tests to check for inherited or genetic conditions, such as sickle cell.

Antenatal support is offered by the following health professionals:

- GP (general practitioner)
- Obstetrician (a doctor specialising in pregnancy, labour and birth)
- Midwife (cares for women before, during and immediately after birth)
- Health visitor (a trained nurse who takes over care ten days after birth).

Where does antenatal care happen?

Antenatal care may be carried out:

- at the hospital where you are due to give birth
- at your GP surgery
- from community midwives at a health centre
- in your own home, where the midwife or doctor visits you
- at another hospital, where there may be special facilities not on offer at your local hospital
- through 'shared care', where appointments are split between your doctor and your hospital.

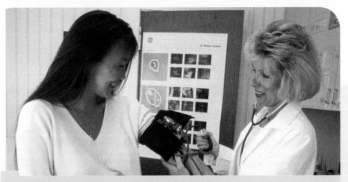

Routine blood pressure check

ROUTINE TESTS

A number of routine tests are carried out at every antenatal visit.

> **Routine tests include checking the following:**
>
> - Blood pressure. It is important that the mother's blood pressure does not get too high as this may lead to pregnancy-induced hypertension (also called pre-eclampsia), which can be harmful to both mother and baby and may cause premature labour. Other symptoms include swollen ankles and gaining too much weight.
> - Examination of the uterus. The uterus is examined by the doctor or midwife, who feels the outside of the abdomen to gain some idea of the baby's size and position.
> - Urine. This is tested for the following:
>   - sugar (glucose) – if present, it may indicate diabetes in the mother
>   - protein – if present, it may indicate an infection of the kidneys or bladder.

OTHER TESTS

A small sample of blood is taken from the mother for a variety of tests at the first visit.

> **Blood samples are needed to check the following:**
>
> - The mother's blood group, in case she needs a blood transfusion at any time.
> - The mother's Rhesus factor. People with this factor are called Rhesus positive and those without the factor are called Rhesus negative. If the mother's blood is Rhesus negative, problems may arise if the baby's father is Rhesus positive. If the baby is Rhesus negative, there is no problem. If the baby is Rhesus positive, the first baby will be all right, but the next Rhesus positive baby could have anaemia, jaundice or developmental problems. Rhesus negative mothers will have their blood tested on giving birth and may need an injection to protect their next baby.
> - If the mother is immune to rubella (German measles).
> - If the mother has anaemia, to establish if her iron levels are appropriate. If iron levels are low she may need an iron supplement.
> - If the mother has syphilis, to detect and treat it. Syphilis can infect the baby.
> - If the mother has Hepatitis B, a virus that causes liver disease and may infect the baby if the mother is a carrier or is infected during pregnancy. The baby can be immunised at birth to prevent infection.

There are also tests available for Hepatitis C and HIV. They are offered if the mother is at risk from either of these viruses. Both tests can be done from the same blood sample. Other tests are available for those at risk of thalassacmia (a red blood cell disorder) and sickle cell anaemia (where the red blood cells change shape).

Foetal heartbeat

After around the twelfth week of pregnancy, the foetal heartbeat can be heard using a Doppler, a sensitive instrument placed on the mother's abdomen.

Ultrasound scans

Ultrasound scans are usually carried out at around weeks 12 and 19 of pregnancy and produce pictures of the baby in the uterus. The first scan provides the following information: the baby's age, position, size, position of the placenta, heartbeat and if there is a multiple pregnancy (more than one baby). The second scan is used to check that the baby is developing normally and may identify some abnormalities.

Down's risk screening test

The Down's test is used to find out the risk of having a baby with **Down's syndrome**. A blood sample is taken between weeks 14 and 20 of pregnancy and the result is available within two weeks. If the mother falls into the high risk group following this test, further tests – such as **amniocentesis** – may be necessary.

AFP test

Using the same blood sample, another test is also available – the **alphafetoprotein (AFP)** test. This test is for screening spina bifida and can be offered to the mother independently from the Down's test if she prefers not to be screened for Down's. Some mothers may decide not to have the AFP test if they are against terminating the pregnancy.

Amniocentesis

This test is used to detect chromosome abnormalities and is usually carried out from week 15 onwards. An ultrasound scan is carried out and a hollow needle is inserted through the abdominal wall into the uterus. Some of the amniotic fluid is removed. There is a risk of miscarriage with this test, and the results take about two to three weeks.

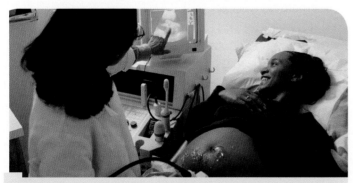

An ultrasound scan provides useful information about the unborn baby

There are several reasons for having amniocentesis:
- the Down's risk screening test has shown a high risk for Down's syndrome
- the mother is older than average, which could increase the risk of Down's syndrome
- the family has a history of inherited chromosome or health problems.

Additional scans

More specialised scans such as 2D and 3D scans and a Nuchal scan are sometimes used to identify higher risks of Down's syndrome in developing babies.

CVS test

The **chorionic villus sampling (CVS)** test involves removing a small sample of placenta tissue during an ultrasound scan, using a hollow needle which is passed through the abdominal wall into the uterus. It is carried out after ten weeks of pregnancy and can detect Down's syndrome. There is a risk of miscarriage with this test, but results may be available within three to four days, which is much quicker than the amniocentesis. The mother has the option of an early termination if the result is abnormal. This test is offered to older mothers or those who have a family history of inherited chromosome and health problems.

The amniocentesis and CVS tests are used for detecting Down's syndrome and, if positive, may result in the pregnancy being terminated.

KEY POINTS

- **An antenatal clinic is where mothers-to-be go for regular testing to ensure they are as well as possible and the baby is developing normally.**
- **Amniocentesis and CVS are both tests which can detect Down's syndrome.**

KEY TASKS

1 Describe the purpose of the following antenatal tests:
  a Blood pressure.   b Uterus.   c Urine.
2 What is the purpose of the first blood test?
3 Why is an ultrasound scan carried out?
4 Describe the amniocentesis test, and why it may be necessary.
5 Explain the risks of not attending regular antenatal check-ups.

Think about it

If a Down's syndrome test is positive should a termination be offered?

Antenatal provision (2)

ANTENATAL CLASSES

As well as attending an antenatal clinic for regular tests, the expectant mother will be advised to attend antenatal classes.

> **At antenatal classes, mothers-to-be learn about:**
> - the development of the unborn baby
> - how to maintain a healthy lifestyle in pregnancy
> - methods of pain relief available during the birth
> - relaxation and breathing exercises
> - breast and bottle feeding
> - how to handle and care for the new baby.

The father-to-be may accompany his partner to antenatal classes for couples, and fathers' evenings are often available. Most men stay with their partner during labour. Antenatal classes are a good opportunity to talk about labour and to complete a birth plan together. The more the father knows about labour, the more he can help and guide the mother. If the father is unavailable, a friend or relative can accompany the mother to antenatal classes instead as a nominated birthing partner. The birthing partner will learn about pregnancy and how to help during the birth, so they will be prepared, will know what to expect and can give encouragement to the mother when she needs it.

Exercises taking place at an antenatal class

There will be the opportunity to ask any questions and meet other expectant parents.

METHODS OF DELIVERY

Most babies are born in hospital, but there are also a number who are born at home. Whether a baby is born at home, or in hospital, it is important that both mother and baby receive the best possible care to ensure a safe delivery.

> **Some mothers are advised to have their baby in hospital, including:**
> - those having their first baby
> - those who have experienced previous problems during birth
> - those who have a history of miscarriage or other pregnancy complications, e.g. diabetes
> - those who are over the age of 35
> - those having a multiple birth
> - those living in poor home conditions, as this may be a health risk to both mother and baby.

Such women are advised to have their babies in hospital so that the best possible facilities are available in case a complication arises during the birth.

Those mothers who do not meet any of the above criteria may have a choice about where to have their baby. They should consider the following information about hospital and home delivery.

> **Advantages of a hospital delivery:**
> - the mother will have the opportunity to talk to other mothers
> - she will be free from household responsibilities, and should have the chance to rest and relax while the baby is asleep
> - special equipment is available should an emergency occur
> - the mother's and baby's health can be monitored throughout labour.
>
> **Disadvantages of a hospital delivery:**
> - the mother will have little privacy
> - she will not know the midwife who is looking after her
> - she may be in unfamiliar surroundings
> - visitors will be restricted to visiting times.

Some mothers who have their baby delivered normally may stay in hospital for only about six hours after the birth. They will then go home, where the community midwife takes care of both the baby and the mother.

Advantages of a home delivery:

- the mother will have more choice when giving birth to her baby at home
- she may have all her family present at the birth
- she will know the midwife and doctor who are looking after her
- she will not be restricted to hospital routines
- she will be able to take care of the baby in her own way.

Disadvantages of a home delivery:

- the mother will not have so much rest as there may be household responsibilities and other children to look after
- she will not have the contact with other mothers
- if a problem occurs during the birth, the mother may need to be taken to hospital
- there may be a lack of specialist monitoring equipment.

Talk about it

- Is there really a choice of where to give birth or are mums persuaded to go to hospital in reality?

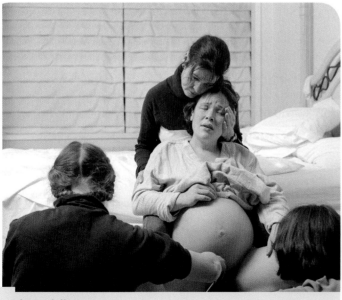

A home delivery

GradeStudio

When answering a question on antenatal care, make sure you are clear about the difference between 'antenatal' and 'postnatal' otherwise many valuable marks could be lost. Remember that 'ante' means before and 'post' means after.

A possible exam question might be:

Visits to the antenatal clinic become more frequent in the last month of pregnancy. Explain the routine checks made on the pregnant mother in this last month when she visits the antenatal clinic.

A good answer will discuss the following checks, which are carried out at every visit:

- blood pressure
- the abdomen and uterus are examined
- urine is checked for presence of sugar and protein.

An excellent answer would go on to explain why each of these checks is needed and the importance of noting changes.

A poor answer would list all checks – including the scans and blood tests which are not routine checks – showing a lack of understanding or misreading of the question.

FURTHER WORK

Investigate the antenatal facilities in your area. Record your findings.

Birth (1)

At around 40 weeks after conception, the baby is ready to be born. The process of giving birth is called **labour**. When labour starts a mother may experience one or more of the following:

- a show – a plug of mucus mixed with blood may come away from the cervix (neck of the uterus), indicating that it is beginning to open

- the breaking of the waters – the amniotic sac containing the amniotic fluid in which the baby has been developing may break, releasing the fluid

- contractions begin – these usually start slowly (every 20 to 30 minutes) and become stronger and more frequent during the first stage of labour.

The onset of labour is usually slow, allowing the mother time to prepare for the birth. Labour is divided into three stages.

STAGE 1

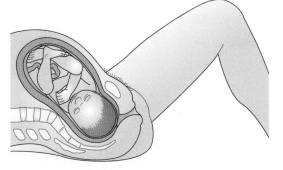

Baby during the first stage of labour

The contractions of the muscles of the uterus wall gradually open the cervix until it is wide enough for the baby's head to pass through (it is fully dilated when it measures 10 cm in diameter). Towards the end of the first stage the contractions may be every two minutes. The first stage is the longest and, for a first baby, can last up to 12 to 18 hours on average.

There are several methods of pain relief which can be used to help the mother through labour and these are discussed on pages 38–39.

If possible, it is easier for the mother if she can walk about during the early part of this stage. During the latter part of this stage each mother will find a position that suits her, for example lying on her side or kneeling on all fours.

STAGE 2

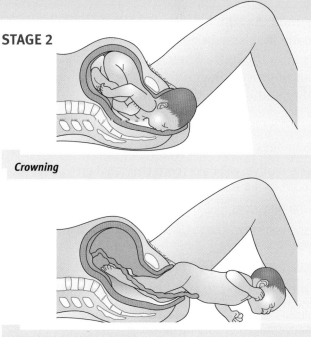

Crowning

Stage 2 is now complete

The cervix will now be fully dilated and the uterus, cervix and vagina have become the **birth canal**. Contractions are very strong and push the baby along the birth canal. The midwife will indicate to the mother when to start pushing and the baby's head will be pushed out from the vagina. This process is called crowning. The midwife will then ease the shoulders out and the baby will be born. Delivery is often onto the mother's abdomen.

Occasionally the vagina does not stretch sufficiently to allow the baby's head to pass through. When this happens, a small cut is needed to widen the opening. This is called an **episiotomy**. The cut is then stitched together after the birth.

STAGE 3

After the birth, the umbilical cord is clamped in two places and a cut is made between them. The contractions continue until the placenta (or afterbirth) is delivered through the vagina. Labour is now complete. The baby is carefully checked at birth and is given to the mother to hold as soon as possible.

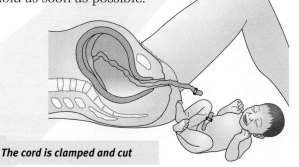

The cord is clamped and cut

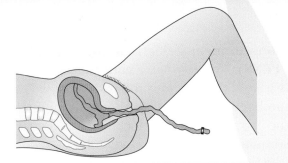

The placenta is delivered through the vagina

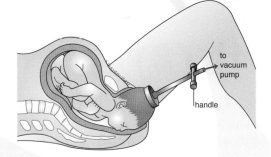

Ventouse delivery

 LINK For more information on postnatal examination see pages 44–45.

COMPLICATIONS DURING BIRTH

Sometimes complications occur during the birth and special treatment may be required in order to deliver the baby.

Breech birth

Babies are usually born head first, but occasionally they are born either feet or bottom first. This is called the **breech position**.

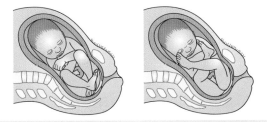

Breech births are either feet first (left) or bottom first (right)

Forceps delivery

A **forceps delivery** may be needed if the baby is in an awkward position or if the mother is becoming exhausted and the contractions are not strong enough to push the baby out.

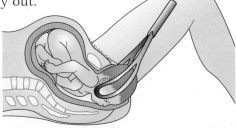

Forceps delivery

Ventouse (suction) delivery

If the delivery is not going as planned, **ventouse** may be necessary. A special cap is connected to a suction pump. The cap is then placed against the head of the baby and a vacuum is created. The doctor or midwife pulls on this until the baby is born.

Caesarian section

An incision is made through the abdominal wall of the uterus so the baby can be delivered. A Caesarian can be carried out under general anaesthetic or using an epidural anaesthetic so that the mother may remain conscious and the birth partner can also be present. Caesarian sections are performed if the birth canal is too small, if the baby is in the breech position or if the health of the baby or mother makes immediate delivery necessary.

Induction

Sometimes labour needs to be started off artificially. This is called **induction**. Labour is induced if the baby is overdue by 14 days or if the baby's or mother's health is at risk.

KEY POINTS

- The process of giving birth is called labour.
- There are three stages of labour.
- Some complications in labour may result in babies needing special assistance or treatment in order to be delivered safely.

KEY TASKS

1 Briefly describe the three stages of labour.
2 What is a Caesarian section and why might it be necessary?
3 Explain the situations when help may be needed with the delivery.

GradeStudio

It is essential to know the three stages of labour and what happens during each. Be really careful not to confuse them. Stage 2 is when the baby is actually born.

Birth (2)

PAIN RELIEF

Labour can be a painful experience for many mothers. Different types of pain relief are available and these are discussed at antenatal classes.

The midwife will give details on all the options of pain relief available so that the mother can consider which one is best for her. It is a difficult decision to make before going into labour as the mother will not know what the pain is going to be like. It is best to have all the methods explained in advance so she can understand what is involved.

Common methods of pain relief

a Relaxation and breathing exercises. These are natural childbirth techniques which help to relieve the pain without any painkillers. These exercises are taught in antenatal classes.

b **Entonox**. This is a mixture of nitrous oxide and oxygen which is breathed through a mask or mouthpiece. It does not harm the baby, but acts quickly and wears off in minutes. Entonox can be used at any time during labour when the mother feels it is necessary, but it may make her feel a little sick or light-headed.

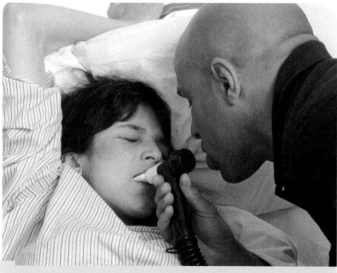

Entonox can help with labour pains

c **Pethidine**. This is an injection that helps you to relax and may lessen the pain. It can make the mother and the baby feel drowsy, which is why it is only given in the early stages of labour. It may also make the mother feel a little sick. As midwives are able to give it without prescription, it can be widely used.

d **Transcutaneous electrical nerve stimulation (TENS)**. This is when a gentle electrical current is passed through four flat pads attached to the mother's back. It has no known harmful effects on the baby. It works by blocking pain signals and by stimulating the body's production of endorphins (the body's natural painkilling substances).

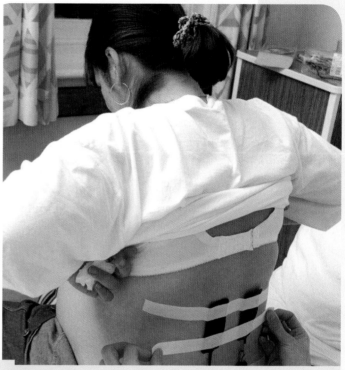

TENS machine

e **Epidural anaesthetic**. This is the most effective method and it has little effect on the baby. It is given through a fine tube inserted into the mother's lower back and numbs the mother from the waist downwards. Mobile epidurals are now available – these allow a small amount of movement, e.g. the mother is able to sit in a chair or possibly, with help, walk to the toilet.

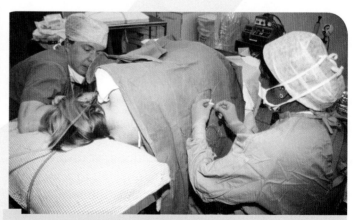

An epidural being administered by an anaesthetist

Alternative methods of pain relief

There are a variety of other methods available in some hospitals that can also be helpful during the early stages of labour. Relaxation is important, and moving around often helps to ease the pain.

The following methods of pain relief may be available in some hospitals, and often the mother can arrange this herself – for example, an aromatherapist to go with her:

- music and aromatherapy – essential oils are massaged into the skin while listening to music
- homeopathy – these remedies are taken from plants and minerals and are used under the advice of a homeopath
- acupuncture – tiny needles are inserted into points on the earlobe, which release the body's natural painkillers. Needles are attached to a TENS machine
- reflexology – the massaging of special zones on the feet can release the body's natural painkillers
- hypnosis or hypnotherapy can be successful in helping the mother to relax.

BIRTH PLANS

A birth plan is a plan of how the mother would like to give birth. It offers the opportunity to think about what she might prefer in advance.

A birth plan can include issues such as:

- where she would like to give birth (at home, in hospital)
- what kind of delivery she would like (in bed, in water)
- who she would like to be present at the birth (husband, partner, mother, friend)
- what delivery position she would like to be in (sitting, standing, squatting)
- the pain relief methods she would prefer (pethidine, epidural, or gas and air).

WATER BIRTHS

A water birth will only be an option if women have a low risk pregnancy where there have been no complications. It is thought to be far less stressful for a baby as they are born into an environment that is similar to the one they were growing in. For the mother it can reduce stress and the need for pain relief. The baby's breathing does not start until he or she is exposed to the air, so the safety risks are minimal.

A water birth is thought to be less stressful for both mother and baby

THE ROLE OF THE FATHER OR BIRTH PARTNER

The father's role throughout labour is important to the mother as he can support and encourage her, as well as being present for the birth of his child. Where the father is unavailable the mother can choose someone close to her to act as her birth partner.

A birth partner can:
- provide company during the labour
- offer comfort, maybe a massage, drinks, etc.
- provide encouragement, reminding the mother of relaxation and breathing techniques.

KEY POINTS

- **Several types of pain relief are available to help the mother during the birth.**
- **Some hospitals offer a range of alternative methods of pain relief.**
- **The father or birth partner is encouraged to take part in the birth.**

KEY TASKS

1 Describe the following methods of pain relief:
   a Entonox.   d TENS.
   b Pethidine.   e Epidural anaesthetic.
   c Relaxation and breathing exercises.
2 Explain the alternative methods of pain relief.
3 Outline the importance of the role of the father or birth partner during labour.
4 Consider the birth options that are available to the mother. Imagine that it is you in this situation. Write your own birth plan.

FURTHER WORK

Design and make a leaflet on the methods of pain relief available for the expectant mother.

Preparing for the baby (1)

It is important for parents and carers to prepare for the physical, social and emotional needs of the new baby to ensure that the baby will be growing within a warm, secure and loving environment.

SOCIAL AND EMOTIONAL NEEDS

Parents and carers need to be aware that babies are influenced by the environment they are brought up in from an early age. Cuddling a baby is very important so that the baby will be comforted and will feel secure. The baby needs to develop feelings of affection. In order for this to take place, he or she needs close contact to establish and form relationships with the people around her or him.

 LINK For more information on emotional development see pages 118–121.

Smiling and talking to the baby is also recognised as being very important for the baby to develop socially. Babies use their eyes and ears to watch and listen to what is going on around them. If the baby is spoken to, she or he will soon respond and interact with that person by smiling and making noises.

LINK For more information on social development see pages 122–123.

Ways of cuddling a newborn baby

Providing toys and things to look at also helps the baby to develop physically and intellectually. A mobile above the cot, pictures on the wall and music to listen to will encourage development.

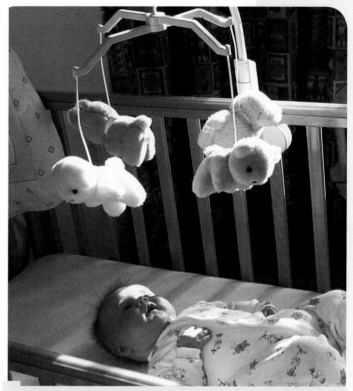

A baby needs stimulus as well as comfort

PHYSICAL NEEDS

Physically, a baby requires both clothing and certain items of nursery equipment. Some of the nursery items allow the baby to react socially and emotionally with family members and others who are around the baby – for example, a high chair at mealtimes allows social interaction to take place.

The first set of baby clothes is often called the layette. Many mothers-to-be enjoy collecting and buying articles of clothing, but a new baby requires only a few.

When buying clothing for a baby, the clothes should be:
- soft
- warm
- loose and comfortable
- washable
- non-irritant (will not irritate the skin)
- flame resistant (will not catch fire easily)
- easy to put on and take off.

Certain types of clothing may be particularly useful.

Some examples of items that may be necessary:

- vests – these are worn next to the skin and made of soft fabric
- stretch suits – all-in-one and enclose the feet
- cardigans – used when an extra layer is needed for warmth
- hat – needed for hot and cold weather
- shawl – warm and lightweight
- socks – to keep the feet warm
- bootees/padders – to keep the feet warm
- sleep suits – needed for warmth on cold nights and made of fleecy fabric
- pram suits – padded, all-in-one suits for outdoor wear.

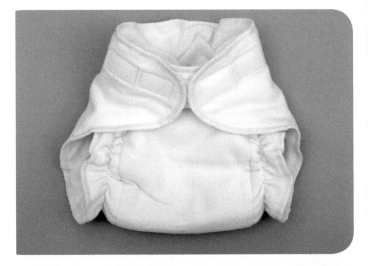

Examples of different nappy types: reusable (top) and disposable (bottom)

Nappies

Nappies also need to be purchased for the new arrival.

There are three different types of nappy:

- Terry nappies – these are made of terry towelling, which is a hard-wearing, absorbent material. Terries are expensive to buy but, once bought, can be used again and again and should last for more than one baby.
- Disposable nappies – these are available in different sizes and are unisex (suitable for a boy or a girl). They save time as they are thrown away instead of being washed, but they are more expensive in the long term. Disposable nappies are non-biological, which means they do not rot down, and therefore are a threat to the environment.
- Reusable nappies – these are becoming more popular and are washable nappies that can be used more than once. They are made of flannelette, have adjustable waistbands and elasticated leg openings, and are lined with absorbent pads.

KEY POINTS

- **Parents and carers need to be well prepared for the arrival of the new baby so that they can provide the appropriate environment.**
- **Parents and carers should be aware that the way they behave and react towards their new baby will influence how the baby develops.**

KEY TASKS

1 Suggest six points to consider when choosing clothing for a new baby.

2 Compare the differences between disposable and terry nappies.

3 Explain how parents and carers can help a newborn baby to develop socially and emotionally in the early days.

4 Explain why it is important for a baby to feel comfortable.

Talk about it

Which types of nappy should new mothers be encouraged to use? Consider the environmental issues and the costs involved with the different types.

Preparing for the baby (2)

As well as clothing, a baby will need several items of equipment to sleep, sit and play in. There is a wide variety of types available, some essential and some non-essential, depending on the expectant couple's lifestyle. The parents and carers need to choose wisely and to buy items that suit their finances. All nursery equipment should carry a kitemark. This is a safety label that shows the equipment has been made to the correct British Standard.

BABY EQUIPMENT

Prams

Prams are available in various styles. Many types can be converted into a carrycot or buggy and many have a car seat/carrying insert – these are the most versatile and economical.

> **Whatever style of pram is bought, it should:**
> - be sturdy and strong
> - have safe brakes
> - be weather resistant
> - be well balanced and easy to steer.

Prams are available in a variety of styles

Pushchairs and buggies

These are most suitable for the older baby or child. A wide variety of combination pram/pushchair buggies are available and these are generally easier for shopping and travelling than a traditional style of pram. They fold for easy storage and to be put into the car or taken on the bus. They may have a wide variety of different features, e.g. a shopping basket, hood and apron or see-through cover for protection against the weather. All types should be fitted with a safety harness for the baby/child to be held in safely.

Baby carriers

Slings and baby carriers are a convenient method of transporting a young baby or older child when buggies or prams are impractical, for example when out walking or in crowded places.

Cots

Cots are almost essential as they provide a safe place for the baby to sleep in.

Cots are almost essential

> **Parents and carers should consider the following points before purchasing a cot:**
> - the bars must be no more than 6 cm apart
> - it should have a well-fitting waterproof mattress with no gaps anywhere.

Cot beds

These are a combination of a cot and a bed. They have an adjustable height mattress and can convert from a cot into a bed by lowering the height of the mattress and removing the slatted sides as the child gets older.

Travel cots

Travel cots are useful items if travelling on holiday or visiting relatives and friends. Some can also be used as a playpen for when the baby is mobile.

Some types of travel cot can also be used as a playpen

Carrycots/moses baskets

These can be used for newborn babies and ensure a warm, snug environment for sleeping.

Bedding

Blankets and sheets should be easy to wash and lightweight. Pillows and duvets should never be used with babies under the age of one year, as there may be a risk of suffocation in a young baby.

A bouncing cradle must always be placed on the ground

Bouncing cradle

A bouncing cradle is useful for a young baby to sit in and take notice of their surroundings. This should not be placed on a high surface, as the chair may fall off. It is only suitable for babies up to a certain weight.

High chair

A high chair is useful so that the older baby (from about six months) can sit at the table with the rest of the family and join in at mealtimes. Some high chairs convert into a low chair and table. A safety harness should always be used in both styles of chair.

A high chair means the baby can join in at mealtimes

Walking reins

Walking reins with a safety harness are essential for toddlers, as they can experience walking skills while remaining under the control of an adult. As the child gets older, reins can be replaced by a strap which attaches to the wrist of both child and adult.

Car seats

Car seats are a legal requirement when the baby is going to be travelling in the car. There is a range of different types and styles available, which are suitable for various ages and stages.

LINK For more information on car seats see page 71.

KEY POINTS

- A selection of clothing and equipment will need to be purchased but care should be taken not to overspend if on a budget.
- Some items of nursery equipment are non-essential but it is up to the parents and carers whether these are purchased.
- Baby baths, playpens and baby bouncers can also be bought and, although these are not essential items, many parents and carers find them useful.

KEY TASKS

1 What points should parents or carers consider when buying the following items of equipment?

  a A pram.

  b A cot.

2 What are the advantages of buying the following pieces of equipment?

  a A travel cot.

  b A bouncing cradle.

  c Walking reins.

  d A high chair.

  e A pushchair/buggie.

3 Analyse which items of equipment are essential and which ones would be desirable. Explain your choices.

Think about it

Is it really necessary to buy all new items of equipment for a new baby?

FURTHER WORK

Investigate the most popular items of nursery equipment and record the cost of these items using ICT.

Postnatal care

The term **postnatal** refers to the days and weeks immediately following the birth of a baby. There are two professionals who look after, advise and support the mother and newborn baby.

THE MIDWIFE

The midwife visits every day until the baby is at least ten days old. If the mother is still in hospital, the midwives there offer support. If the mother is at home, the community midwife visits on a daily basis. Both mother and baby are checked at every visit to ensure they are progressing well.

THE HEALTH VISITOR

The health visitor takes over from the midwife after about ten days and may visit for up to six weeks after that. Alternatively, the mother may see the health visitor at the baby clinic, which is usually held on the same day each week at the nearest health centre.

Health visitors undertake the following role:

- provide support and promote good health for both baby and mother
- answer any questions and concerns
- advise on immunisations
- weigh the baby regularly to check progress
- keep checks on the baby's developmental progress
- provide opportunities for mothers to meet and share experiences with other new mothers.

Health visitors offer support to both mother and baby

EXAMINATION OF THE BABY

The day following the birth, the baby will be examined by a doctor who will carry out the following examinations:

- checks the baby's eyes
- listens to the heart
- checks the number of fingers and toes
- checks the mouth for a cleft palate – this is where the roof of the mouth has not formed properly and a small operation will be required
- checks for congenital dislocation of the hip – the hip joints are tested for movement and treatment is necessary if the hip is dislocated to prevent permanent damage.

THE NEO-NATAL SCREENING TEST

This involves taking a sample of blood from the baby at around the sixth day after the birth. The baby's heel is pricked to collect the sample.

The baby's blood is tested for three conditions:

- Phenylketonuria (PKU). This is a rare disorder that is caused by an enzyme deficiency which leaves the baby unable to use an acid present in milk and other foods. If left untreated, PKU can affect the baby's mental development and he or she could become mentally handicapped. Treatment involves putting the baby on a special diet.
- Congenital hypothyroidism. The thyroid gland (situated just below the voice box) may be missing or not functioning correctly. This slows down physical and mental development, resulting in children being undersized and having learning difficulties. Treatment involves taking the thyroid hormone thyroxine.
- Cystic fibrosis. This is a disorder that gives rise to chronic lung disease. There is no complete cure as yet, but if early treatment can be given the child can be helped to grow up physically stronger.

UMBILICAL CORD

The stump of the baby's umbilical cord dries, shrivels and drops off within seven to ten days following the birth.

VITAMIN K

It is recommended that all babies are given an injection of vitamin K within the first 24 hours of birth. Vitamin K is essential in the blood-clotting process.

THE MOTHER

At around six weeks after the birth, the mother has a postnatal examination. This is carried out by either the hospital or the family doctor. The mother is examined to ensure she is healthy and that her uterus has returned to normal. The baby is also examined to make sure normal progress is being made.

The mother is encouraged to carry out gentle postnatal exercises to help tighten the abdominal muscles and the muscles of the pelvic floor (muscles in the groin which can be controlled when passing urine and which have been stretched during pregnancy and birth).

POSTNATAL DEPRESSION

In the first few weeks following the birth, it is common for the mother to experience 'highs and lows'. She may be tearful or feel down and depressed. This is known as the 'baby blues' and, with support and help from family and midwives, these feelings should pass within a few days.

> Reasons for the 'baby blues' may include:
> * hormonal changes
> * lack of sleep because of disturbed nights
> * the mother feeling she has no time for herself.

However, if these feelings develop into long-term depression this is more serious, and requires advice and help from the doctor.

THE FATHER

The father's role immediately after the birth is very important in giving him time to get to know his baby, supporting the mother, helping with household tasks and sharing the care of the baby. It is possible for him to obtain paternity leave (time off from work) of up to two weeks.

NEEDS OF THE WHOLE FAMILY

The birth of a new baby has a dramatic effect on all members of the family. Tiredness caused by disturbed nights can result in a lack of patience with other family members. It is important to consider the feelings of other children and to include them in the preparation for, and care of, the new baby in order to prevent any unnecessary jealousy. Having a new addition to the family is expensive and careful

It is important for a father to bond with his baby in the first few weeks

budgeting may be required. Also, it is important to make existing children feel included when visitors come to see the new baby.

REGISTRATION OF THE BIRTH

The baby needs to be registered by the parents within six weeks of the birth. The child's name must be given to the registrar before a birth certificate can be issued.

KEY POINTS

* The midwife is responsible for the welfare of the mother and baby for the first ten days after the birth.
* The health visitor then takes over and is responsible for the baby's developmental progress and well-being.
* The mother should have a postnatal examination six weeks after the birth to ensure she is healthy.
* The father's support is invaluable at this time, and the whole family needs to feel included.

KEY TASKS

1 Describe the role of the health visitor.
2 Explain the neo-natal screening test.
3 What do you understand by the term 'baby blues'?
4 Why is it important to ensure that all new mothers receive good-quality postnatal care?

Talk about it

Discuss ways to help an older sibling feel included when a new baby arrives.

ExamCafé

Unit 2

I like to see things in diagram form. I found it really easy to arrange the information on the stages of labour into a diagram like this one.

Charlie

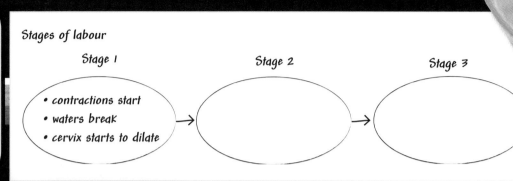

Stages of labour

Stage 1
- contractions start
- waters break
- cervix starts to dilate

Stage 2

Stage 3

This one is started – create one of your own to help you remember the sequence.

I really enjoyed our lesson today as everyone made up three questions to ask the others in the class. There were 22 in the class so that was 66 revision questions in minutes!
This is a brilliant idea and you can cover lots of revision that way.

Georgie

I like colourful things so I use a colour-coding system. It really helps me to organise the information I need to remember. For example, I used green to shade everything in my notes that was to do with antenatal work and pink for everything to do with birth. Blue was for postnatal information. I found it much easier to remember the information that way.

Susie

Revision checklist

Things I really need to remember…

Unit 2 revision checklist: dos and don'ts of pregnancy		
Things to eat regularly	• Dairy foods for calcium, e.g. milk, cheese, yoghurt • Protein-rich foods, e.g. oily fish, lean meat, eggs, pulses • Iron-rich foods, e.g. green vegetables, red meat • Foods rich in folic acid, e.g. broccoli, Marmite	☐☐☐☐
Foods to avoid	• Soft cheeses, e.g. Brie • Raw eggs or products containing them • Liver and pâté • Under-cooked meat, especially chicken	☐☐☐☐
Substances to avoid	• Medicines or drugs of any kind • Alcohol • Smoking • Aromatherapy oils	☐☐☐☐
Diseases to avoid	• Rubella (German measles) • Toxoplasmosis (from litter trays) • Chickenpox	☐☐☐
Things to do	• Get lots of rest • Take regular exercise	☐☐

Common mistakes

Don't confuse the two different types of twins!

Identical
- One placenta which they share
- Always the same sex – both boys or both girls
- Also called uniovular

Non-identical
- Two placentas (one each)
- Could be 2 girls or 2 boys or one of each sex
- Also called binovular, unidentical or fraternal

Revision techniques

Routine tests
Weight gain
Blood pressure
Uterus/abdomen examination
Urine test for sugar – diabetes
Urine test for protein – infection of the kidneys or bladder/ pre-eclampsia

Other tests
Blood group
Blood rhesus factor
Immunity to rubella (German measles)
Iron levels
Hepatitis B
HIV
Hepatitis C
Down's syndrome
AFP
Amniocentesis
CVS

When I am revising I like to write things out as lists. I organise the information first, then list all of the points I need to know. I can then read through them time after time to help me remember the facts.

Hannah

Here's a revision spider diagram on the signs of pregnancy:

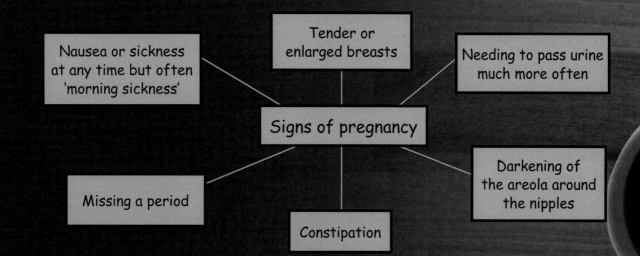

ExamCafé

Here are some Unit 2 sample exam questions, with answers and comments, to help you think about what is required when you are sitting in the exam room!

Question 1

a Which type of twins develop from one egg? **(1 mark)**

Identical twins develop from one egg.

Examiner says:
Correct answer with sufficient detail given. Could also have said uniovular twins.

b Which type of twins could also be called 'fraternal twins'? **(1 mark)**

Non-identical twins can also be called fraternal twins.

Examiner says:
Suitable answer to gain the mark given. Could also have said binovular or unidentical twins.

c Identify the usual number of chromosomes in a fertilised egg. **(1 mark)**

23

Examiner says:
0 marks awarded. The candidate could have said *23 pairs* of chromosomes or *46 chromosomes*. The full phrase is necessary to ensure the examiner knows what you mean and can give you the mark for the answer.

Question 2

Visits to the antenatal clinic happen more often during the last month of a pregnancy.

Explain what the routine checks are that are done at these visits.

(8 marks)

Read through the answer to question 2 below and think how many marks you would give it before you read the examiner's comments.

Student answer

It is really important that the mother remembers to go for her appointments in case her baby is not ok. They will do a scan to see if the baby is a boy or a girl and she might want to know what it is or she may not want to. They will also do a blood test to find out her blood group in case she needs a blood transfusion if it's a difficult birth. The other thing that they do is to see if she is anaemic as that isn't good for her or the baby and they will both be very tired all of the time. She shouldn't be putting on too much weight because it isn't good for her or the baby to get too fat or she could find it difficult and very uncomfortable so they will weigh her to make sure she has not put too much on since the last visit. If they think that there is a risk that the baby might have Down's syndrome they will also do the amniocentesis test to find out.

Examiner says:
The answer the student gave is worth only 1 mark. The student probably thought that she had made a good attempt to answer the question and would get a much higher mark. So what is wrong with the answer that this student has given?
The only correct point that she answered was the point about weighing the mother at every visit. The other points are either completely wrong or the checks that she was suggesting are not routine ones carried out at each appointment.
A scan is usually done at about 12 weeks and again at about 19 weeks. One is certainly not carried out routinely at each visit and would be specifically arranged if needed. An amniocentesis test is never done routinely and would only be done in cases where it is felt to be really necessary, as there are some risks involved.
Blood tests are done much earlier in the pregnancy so that all the required details are recorded in case any problems are detected. They are not routine at each visit.
A much better answer would have been the one on the next page:

Model answer

Checks carried out on the mother when she attends for her antenatal appointments are: to take her blood pressure to monitor it carefully, as high blood pressure can be a sign of pre-eclampsia; and to weigh her to make sure that she has not put on far too much weight as very high gains can lead to high blood pressure and swelling in the late stages of the pregnancy, plus the extra weight is also very difficult to lose later. A urine sample is tested to see if there is any sign of glucose in the sample as this can be a sign of diabetes which sometimes develops during pregnancy and which can be damaging. The sample will also be tested for traces of protein. Protein in the urine can indicate the onset of pre-eclampsia or it may be due to an infection that can easily be treated. The mother's abdomen would be measured to check that the baby is growing at the expected rate. If it is not, it can be a sign that there is something wrong. The heartbeat of the baby will be checked to make sure that the baby is not distressed. It is also a good opportunity for the mother to ask questions and to discuss any worries that she has with the midwife.

Key words	
alphafetoprotein (AFP)	a blood test for screening spina bifida
amniocentesis	a test that uses a hollow needle to remove amniotic fluid
amniotic sac	the sac in which the growing foetus develops
antenatal	before birth
birth canal	the uterus, cervix and vagina
breech position	when the legs or bottom of a baby are presenting first
Caesarean section	a surgical procedure to delivery a baby
chorionic villus sampling (CVS)	a test that removes a sample of the placenta
Down's syndrome	a genetic condition caused by an extra chromosome in the cells
embryo	the fertilised egg after implantation
entonox	nitrous oxide and oxygen ('gas and air') given as pain relief during labour
epidural anaesthetic	pain relief during labour, which blocks nerve signals in and around the mother's spinal cord
episiotomy	a small cut during labour to widen the vaginal opening
foetus	the embryo becomes a foetus after eight weeks
forceps delivery	using an instrument that fits around the baby's head to ease it out during birth
induction	starting off labour artificially
labour	the process of giving birth
lanugo	fine, downy hair covering the body of a foetus
menstruation	the flow of blood that occurs as a monthly period
pethidine	pain relief during labour, given in the form of an injection
placenta	the organ that provides nourishment and removes waste for the foetus
postnatal	refers to the days and weeks after the birth
transcutaneous electrical nerve stimulation (TENS)	a device that blocks pain signals during labour
umbilical cord	contains blood vessels that carry blood and waste products between the placenta and the foetus
ventouse	a cap that is connected to a suction pump, which helps deliver a baby

The newborn baby

'Neo-natal' is the term used for the first week after the birth. When a baby is born, body measurements are taken straight afterwards.

> **The three measurements normally recorded for a newborn are:**
> - weight – the average weight of a full-term baby is 3.5 kg (7.5 lb)
> - length – the average length is 50 cm (20 inches)
> - head circumference – the average measurement around the head is about 35 cm (13.5 inches).

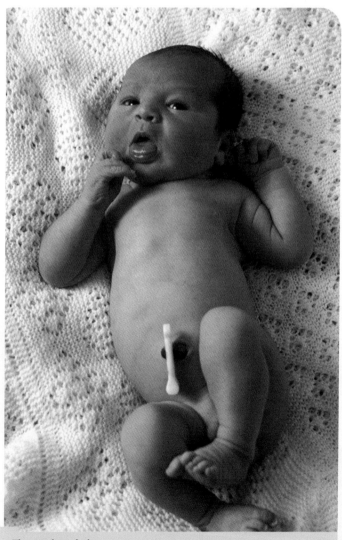

The newborn baby

CHARACTERISTICS OF A NEWBORN BABY

The colour and amount of hair on a newborn baby varies. Some have hardly any hair; others have a large amount. Babies can see when they are born, but they are short-sighted. Fingernails and toenails are present at birth. The head is more developed than the body and is big compared to the rest of the body. On top of the head is a 'soft spot' called the **fontanelle**. This is where the four bones that make up part of the skull have not yet joined together. It will take 12–18 months for the bones to fuse.

At birth the baby's skin is covered in a greasy, white substance called **vernix**.

A number of babies develop mild **jaundice** around the second or third day after birth. This causes the skin and eyes to be tinged yellow. This may clear up on its own within three or four days but it may be necessary to put the baby under ultraviolet lights for a day or two.

Some babies are born with birthmarks. Many of these may disappear over a period of time, but others may be with the child for life.

REFLEX ACTIONS

A newborn baby shows several **reflex actions**. These are movements which are automatic. They are caused by the baby's senses being stimulated. They disappear within three months of birth.

Immediately after birth, a newborn baby is examined by a doctor. The doctor or midwife will test the following reflex actions.

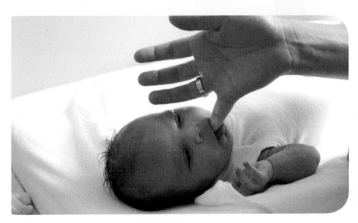

The sucking reflex – a baby will suck on anything that is put into his or her mouth.

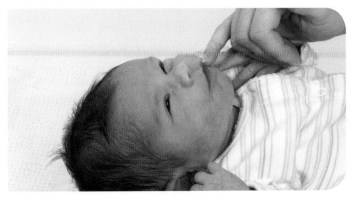

The rooting reflex – if one side of the baby's cheek is touched, the baby's head will turn towards it searching for the mother's nipple.

The stepping reflex – when held upright with the feet on a flat surface, the baby will make forward stepping movements.

The startle reflex – if startled by a sudden loud noise or bright light, the baby will move arms outwards with elbows bent and hands clenched.

The falling ('Moro') reflex – sudden movements that affect the neck give the baby the feeling that it may be dropped, so the baby will fling out the arms and open the hands as if falling.

The grasp reflex – if the palm of the hand is touched with an object or finger, the hand automatically grasps it.

KEY POINTS

- A newborn baby has a 'soft spot' on the head called the fontanelle.
- Newborn babies have many characteristics – along with reflex actions – that all disappear in a relatively short time after birth.

KEY TASKS

1 What is the average weight of a newborn baby?
2 Describe the fontanelle.
3 List the six reflex actions of a newborn baby.
4 Which three measurements are recorded straight after birth?
5 Explain the purpose of examining the baby to test its reflexes.

Think about it

How big (or small!) was the smallest baby that you have had any contact with? Do you know how to hold a new baby?

The needs of a newborn baby

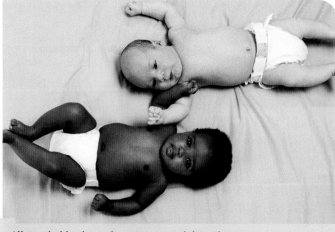

All new babies have the same essential needs

All newborn babies have the same basic needs in order to live, grow and develop in the best possible conditions.

> **All newborn babies need:**
> - warmth
> - protection
> - food
> - sleep
> - love
> - security.

WARMTH

A newborn baby cannot control its own body temperature and can quickly become very hot or very cold. This means they need to be kept in constant, warm conditions. The baby's room should be kept at around 18°C. In an unheated, cold room a baby's body temperature can drop dramatically. On the other hand, a baby can also quickly overheat if it has too many layers of clothing or bedding. Parents need to be vigilant and to be aware of the temperature around the baby.

PROTECTION

A newborn baby needs to be protected and kept safe. This means, for example, not leaving a baby outside a shop, even for a minute, in case of unwanted attention from strangers. Babies are vulnerable and cannot protect themselves, so others must do it for them.

LINK For more information on protection see pages 66–73.

FOOD

A baby needs food in the form of milk and may be either breast or bottle fed. Several feeds a day are required.

LINK For more information on feeding see pages 78–83.

SLEEP

Most newborn babies spend a lot of time asleep, waking only to be fed. Others may be awake for longer periods. The pattern of sleep is not regular at first, but as the baby becomes more aware of daytime and everyday noises the pattern becomes more regular.

The position of sleeping is very important. It is advised that babies sleep on their backs until they are old enough to turn over on their own.

A **cot death** (sudden infant death syndrome or SIDS) is the sudden and unexpected death of a baby for no obvious reason. It can happen after the baby has been put in the cot to sleep, although it can also happen in a pram, the car or even in someone's arms. In recent years the number of cot deaths has fallen.

> **To protect a baby against cot death, parents and carers should follow this advice:**
> - cut smoking in pregnancy (fathers too)
> - place the baby on its back to sleep ('back to sleep')
> - do not let anyone smoke in the same room as the baby
> - do not let the baby get too hot (or too cold)
> - keep the baby's head uncovered – place it with its feet to the foot of the cot
> - sleep the baby in a cot in the same room as you for the first six months
> - do not fall asleep with the baby while sitting or lying on a sofa
> - do not share a bed with the baby
> - do not use a pillow or cot bumpers
> - settle the baby to sleep (day and night) with a dummy
> - seek prompt medical advice if the baby is unwell.

Cot death can happen to any baby, but **premature babies**, **low birth-weight babies** and boys are more at risk. It is more likely at night, between midnight and 9 a.m.

LOVE AND SECURITY

Close contact is important for a newborn baby. **Bonding** is the unconditional love between parents and their child. It should develop through close skin and eye contact in the early weeks of life.

CRYING

Crying is a baby's way of communicating to others that they they need something.

Babies cry for a number of reasons:

- thirst
- sudden noises
- hunger
- discomfort
- tiredness
- boredom
- pain
- loneliness
- dislike of the dark.

Babies cry for a variety of reasons

Whatever the reason for crying, a baby should never be left to cry for too long. Making soothing noises, using a low voice, or playing soft music often calms a baby. Gentle rocking and a massage may also soothe a restless baby.

PREMATURE BABIES

A premature baby (pre-term) is one born before 37 weeks of pregnancy or a full-term low birth-weight baby weighing less than 2.5 kg (5.5 lb).

Premature babies need special care as they may have problems with:

- breathing
- sucking
- maintaining their own body temperature (keeping warm).

Incubators

A premature baby is kept in an **incubator** from birth. An incubator is an apparatus that can be seen through and acts like the uterus for the under-developed baby. The incubator also keeps the baby isolated and offers protection.

The incubator provides the baby with:

- oxygen to help with breathing problems
- a tube that will supply its food
- constant humidity and temperature control.

Parents and carers are encouraged to play a part in caring for their premature baby in order to allow bonding to take place.

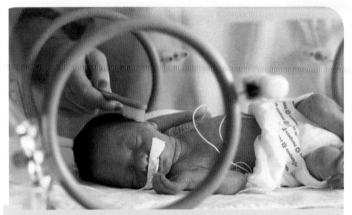

A premature baby in an incubator

KEY POINTS

- The needs of a newborn baby are basic, but very demanding for parents and carers, who will find that caring for a baby is a 24-hour job.
- Babies who are born prematurely require special care and attention, as well as all the basic needs.

KEY TASKS

1 What are the basic needs of a newborn baby?
2 Why is it advisable that newborn babies sleep on their backs?
3 Explain the problems that a premature baby may experience and how they can be corrected.
4 Suggest some reasons why a baby may be born prematurely.

Talk about it

All new babies are very time consuming, so imagine having twins or triplets!

- Discuss the needs of newly born triplets.
- Work out a plan of how to cope with the babies.

Stages of development (1)

Physical development is the development of the body and the way the child acquires skills as it progresses. Throughout the sections on development, the term **milestones** or development norms will be referred to, as well as the ages of children. Milestones of development are a way of assessing the progress of a baby/child and are used to monitor development.

Developmental screening tests are carried out at regular intervals at a health clinic, GP's surgery or by the health visitor. This involves observing the child in a series of tests.

The ages suggested are the average ages of children and it is normal for there to be variations in their developmental progress. They are to be used only as a rough guide.

> **The normal progression of development depends on various factors:**
> - the genes the child has inherited
> - the health of the child
> - the environment in which the child is brought up
> - the stimulation and encouragement provided by the parents.

There are two areas of physical development:

a **Gross motor skills**, which involve the use of the large muscles in the body and include activities such as walking, running and climbing.

b **Fine manipulative skills**, which involve the precise use of the hands and fingers, such as pointing, drawing, writing, fastening buttons or shoelaces.

Physical development includes sensory development – the development of the five senses: sight, touch, hearing, smell and taste. All these senses are important to a child as it develops. Here we are going to look at sight and hearing.

 LINK For more information on gross motor and fine manipulative skills see pages 56–61.

SIGHT

Babies can focus on their father's face

At birth, babies can see but they cannot focus on objects further than 25 cm away. They are aware of light, darkness and movement and can focus on the mother's or carer's face, for example during feeding.

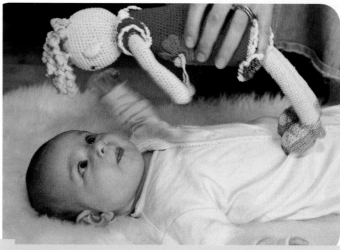
Eyes following a moving toy

At around three months the baby is still short-sighted but can see further. At this age, the baby's eyes will follow people or objects nearby and the baby spends a lot of time looking at its own hands.

At about six months, the eyes begin to work together and babies will start to reach out for objects. By one year, babies can recognise people at a distance, and at 18 months they realise they are looking at themselves in a mirror. By the age of two and a half years, children can recognise themselves in photographs and by the age of three years they have developed all the visual skills of an adult. At four years a child can match and name four primary colours and by five years can match ten to twelve colours. Until they start school, a child's eyesight is checked at regular intervals in order to establish that normal progress is being made. Any problems with eyesight can be identified early on and treatment and/or specialist help can then be provided.

HEARING

Even before birth, research tells us that babies respond to loud noises in the mother's uterus. A newborn baby can recognise the parent's or carer's voice and is startled by loud noises. By three months the baby can respond to its name being called and by six months will turn towards a sound, for example their parent's or carer's voice at a distance. At 12 months the baby will recognise familiar sounds and voices, and will know and respond immediately to its own name.

By two years of age it will listen to general conversation with interest. By the age of four years a child can listen to long stories and by five years a child can hear accurately.

Turning in response to hearing her name

Hearing tests are part of normal developmental screening tests. The development of hearing is an essential part of speech (language) development, and any problems with hearing should be identified as early as possible in order to provide treatment or specialist help so that the child may develop as normally as possible.

 KEY POINTS

- Development norms are the same as milestones.
- Physical development involves two main areas called gross motor skills and fine manipulative skills.
- The development of the five senses is called sensory development.
- Hearing and vision development are checked regularly to identify any problems as early as possible.

 KEY TASKS

1 What is meant by the term 'milestone'?
2 Describe what a baby can see at birth.
3 Why is it important that a baby's hearing is checked regularly?
4 Name two factors on which a child's developmental progress depends.
5 a What do you understand by the term fine manipulative skills?
   b Suggest three ways a parent or carer could encourage these skills in a six-month-old baby.

FURTHER WORK

Design and make a mobile to hang over a baby's cot to encourage sensory development (Possible practical short task).

GradeStudio

You need to be aware of what children should be able to do at different ages and stages of development. Try to learn these facts as you go along to help you build up a bank of knowledge to help you to answer questions like these:

1 At between six and nine months a baby will begin to sit unsupported. Suggest four toys that could help develop fine manipulative skills.

2 Learning to sit is a gross motor skill that a baby may acquire during its first year of life. Name three other gross motor skills.

Stages of development (2)

DEVELOPMENT OF MOVEMENT

Movement of the body requires the co-ordination of the brain cells with the muscles in the body. Messages from the brain make the muscles work and then the baby will acquire the necessary skills. There is a certain order in which these skills are acquired. Head control is the first to be learned, followed by the upper body, arms and hand movements and finally the legs.

GROSS MOTOR SKILLS

Head control

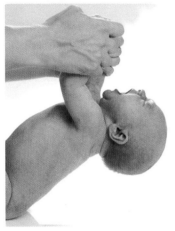

Newborn babies have neck muscles that are weak and they cannot support their heads. When someone is holding the baby, it is important that the head is well supported.

When pulled into a sitting position, a newborn baby's head falls backwards.

At three months the baby has developed some head control and, when pulled into a sitting position, there is little head lag (falling backwards).

By six months the baby has full head control, can use the shoulders to pull itself into a sitting position and can turn the head towards a sound.

Sitting up

In a newborn baby, the muscles in the back are not developed and so the baby cannot sit up.

By three months the baby can sit with a straighter back if held or supported.

At six months the baby can sit upright with a straight back, but will still need support from someone holding their hands in front or using a cushion or chair behind.

Lying on the stomach (prone position)

A newborn baby will lie with the knees brought up under the abdomen, if placed on its front.

At three months the baby can lift both the head and chest off the floor using the forearms for support.

By six months, when lying on the stomach, the baby can lift the head and chest using its hands and straightened arms as support. At around this age the baby will also start rolling over.

The baby at nine months can find ways of moving about the floor, e.g. crawling on the stomach.

At one year the baby can crawl on its hands and knees, shuffling along on its bottom or bear walking (using hands and feet to move).

Most babies crawl before they can walk, but some miss out this stage altogether. This shows the wide variation of normal progression through physical development.

Standing and walking

In order to walk, the muscles in the legs and back need to strengthen and the baby has to learn to keep balance and to co-ordinate all the muscles that are used for walking.

By six months the baby can support almost all its weight and, if held in a standing position, can do so with a straight back.

At nine months the baby can pull itself into a standing position and can stand and take a few steps while holding on to furniture or someone's hands.

At one year the baby can walk with one hand held. By 13 months, some babies can walk alone but they may not have good balance. At 15 months, most babies can walk alone and can crawl up stairs, although some may have difficulty in coming down stairs backwards.

By 18 months the child can walk steadily and stop without sitting down or falling over suddenly. A child of this age will also be able to climb up and down stairs if supported by a rail and by putting both feet on each step. At this age the child will also be able to crawl backwards down the stairs in a safe manner.

At two years the child can run safely, climb onto furniture, throw a ball, walk up and down stairs using both feet on each step, sit on a tricycle and move it with their feet (not pedals). They can also push large toys with wheels and kick a ball.

By two and a half years the child can tiptoe and jump with both feet together.

At three years the child can ride a tricycle using pedals, can catch a large ball with arms outstretched and can go up stairs one foot at a time (but still come down stairs putting two feet on each step).

By four years of age the child can walk up and down stairs like an adult, ride a tricycle with skill, and catch, kick and bounce a ball.

By the age of five years the child can skip, stand on one foot, hop and demonstrate good co-ordination when playing games.

KEY POINTS

- Gross motor skills include activities such as head control, sitting up, crawling and walking.
- Children develop at different rates and it must be remembered that they all go through these stages of physical development in their own time.

KEY TASKS

1 Why is it important that a newborn baby's head is always supported?

2 What is the average age that a baby acquires the following skills?

 a Full head control.

 b Walking alone.

 c Climbing stairs using a handrail for support.

 d Riding a tricycle using the pedals.

3 Describe the likely actions of a baby aged eight to nine months playing with a soft ball on the floor. What would you expect to see the baby do?

GradeStudio

Gross motor skills are about movement and mobility and the development of the large muscles. You need to know what should be expected at each stage to help you to answer the questions in the exam.

Stages of development (3)

FINE MANIPULATIVE SKILLS

A newborn baby has an automatic reflex action called the grasp reflex.

📖 **LINK** For more information on newborn reflex actions see pages 50–51.

By three months the baby will start to control the hands, will spend time playing with his or her hands and may hold a rattle for a short time.

At six months the baby can grasp an object, using the whole hand to pass a toy from one hand to the other.

At nine months the fingers and thumb are used to grasp an object. This is known as the pincer grasp. At around four weeks later, the baby can pick up small objects with the finger and thumb.

At one year the baby can point with the index finger and place one brick on top of another. By 15 months, the baby can show a preference for one hand over the other and can grasp a crayon using a whole hand grasp.

At 18 months the child can build a tower of three to five bricks, scribble a picture, use a spoon for feeding (messily) and hold a pencil in the whole hand or with the thumb and first two fingers tripod grasp.

The child of two years can build a tower of six or more bricks, draw circles, lines and dots, drink from a cup, turn single pages in a book and, by two and a half years, can build a tower of seven or more bricks and paint a picture.

At three years of age the child can build a tower of about nine or ten bricks, control a pencil well with the thumb and first two fingers, thread large beads onto a lace, use a fork and spoon to eat with, use scissors to cut paper and draw a person with a head and sometimes legs.

By four years the child can thread small beads onto a lace, hold and use a pencil as an adult, and draw a figure with head, legs and body.

At the age of five years the child can use a knife and fork for eating, sew large stitches, do jigsaw puzzles, has acquired good pencil control and can draw a person with head, body, legs, arms, nose, mouth and eyes.

HAND–EYE CO-ORDINATION

The development of **hand–eye co-ordination** is the ability to connect the movement of the hands with what the eyes can see – the brain controls the muscle movement. Hand–eye co-ordination develops alongside the development of gross motor skills and fine manipulative skills, e.g. a child playing on a climbing frame needs to use his or her eyes to identify where to place hands and feet to tell the brain where to move the limbs.

THE DEVELOPMENT OF TEETH

When a baby is born, the teeth are already developing in the gums. The average age when teeth begin to emerge is at six months. These teeth are called milk teeth. There will be 20 teeth when they have all come through by the age of three years. Milk teeth usually come through in a certain order.

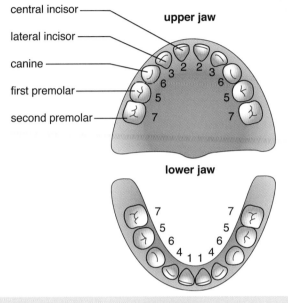

The order in which milk teeth usually appear

After the age of five years the milk teeth begin to fall out as the roots disappear. At the age of six years permanent teeth begin to emerge.

Teething

Teething happens when the teeth emerge through the gums.

A baby may display a number of signs that teething is taking place:

- chewing on hard objects
- excessive dribbling
- fretfulness
- sore gums or a red cheek.

The parent or carer can help to soothe these teething problems by:

- providing hard foods to chew on, e.g. carrot
- cuddling and comforting the baby
- diverting the baby's attention, e.g. playing with a toy or going out.

However, if the baby is very fretful the parent or carer should seek medical advice.

Caring for the teeth

As a rule, sweet, sticky foods should be avoided as they encourage tooth decay. The diet should include foods that are high in calcium to encourage healthy teeth, e.g. milk and cheese, and foods that require chewing, e.g. apples and crusts of bread.

The teeth should be cleaned as soon as they appear, using a small amount of toothpaste and a piece of soft fabric such as muslin. Once the child is one year old they can be given a toothbrush and taught to clean the teeth in an up and down action. Teeth should be cleaned after meals and at bed time. It is important to establish a good teeth cleaning habit early on so it will be continued throughout life.

The dentist

Children should be encouraged to visit the dentist from around the age of three. In this way the child will become used to going and will feel confident about these visits as they get older.

KEY POINTS

- Fine manipulative skills mean the development and control of the hands and the fingers.
- Hand–eye co-ordination is the ability to connect hand movement with what the eyes can see.
- Caring for a child's teeth is important in preventing tooth decay.

KEY TASKS

1 What is the average age that a baby acquires the following skills?
  a Demonstrates the pincer grasp.
  b Builds a tower of three to five bricks.
  c Uses scissors to cut paper.
  d Threads small beads.
2 How many milk teeth does an average 3-year-old have?
3 Suggest two signs that a baby may be teething.
4 Plan the meals for a day for a 2-year-old that will encourage the development of healthy teeth. Give detailed explanations for your choices.

FURTHER WORK

1 Design and make a toy to encourage a fine manipulative skill. Consider the safety of the toy.
2 Design and make a poster to encourage children to clean their teeth.

Physical development milestones (birth to 5 years)

Age	Fine manipulative skills	Gross motor skills	Vision/sight	Hearing
Newborn (called a neonate for the first month)	• Grasp reflex • Fists clenched	• Stepping reflex • Lies in curled position • Head needs support • Head falls back when pulled to a sitting position (head lag)	• Can focus only 15–25 cm away • Stares at brightly coloured objects in range • Focuses on close faces when feeding	• Recognises parent's/carer's voice • Startled by loud noises
3 months	• Plays with hands • Can hold an object, e.g. rattle, for a short time	• Has some head control but head still wobbly • Lifts head and chest off the floor using forearms for support	• Uses eyes to follow objects or nearby people	• Responds to name being called
6 months	• Grasps an object, using the whole hand (palmar grasp)	• Full head control • Can turn head and look around • Sits upright with a straight back but needs support • Lifts head and chest using hands and straight arms • Rolls over	• Eyes work together • Reaches out for things	• Turns toward sounds, especially familiar voices
9 months	• Uses pincer grasp with index finger and thumb	• Sits unsupported for a while and turns the body • May start to move around, e.g. by crawling • Pulls itself into standing position • May try to take a few steps while holding on for support	• Able to focus on a more distant object and may move towards it	• May listen for more distant sounds

1 year	• Uses mature pincer grasp and releases held objects • Points with index finger • Claps hands	• Sits up from lying down position • May crawl, bottom shuffle or bear walk • Can usually walk around furniture or with hand held	• Recognises people at a distance	• Recognises familiar sounds and voices
18 months	• Builds a tower of 3–5 bricks • Uses a spoon for feeding • Holds a pencil in whole hand; tripod grasp is developing	• Walks steadily • May walk up or down stairs with hand held or support • Likes to push a baby walker	• Realises s/he is looking at her/himself in a mirror	• Listens to sounds more intently
2–3 years	• Holds pencil using tripod grasp • Uses a fine pincer grasp to pick up and put things down • Starting to use preferred hand	• Rides a push-along toy not using pedals • Kicks a ball • Throws a ball • Stops and starts with control • Can stand and walk on tiptoe	• Recognises itself in photographs	• Listens to general conversation with interest
4 years	• Grasps a pencil in an adult manner and has good control • Practises zips and buttons • Builds a tower of bricks • Threads small beads	• Rides a tricycle using pedals • Climbs well • Can run on tiptoe • Improved balance • Catches, kicks and bounces a ball	• Matches and names primary colours	• Listens to long stories
5 years	• Has good control of pencils and paint brushes • Uses a knife and fork • Draws people	• Hops, skips and balances on one foot • Plays ball games well • Moves to music with rhythm	• Matches and names 10–12 colours	• Hears accurately

Clothing and footwear for babies and children

There is a wide variety of clothing available for children and there are certain factors to consider when buying these items for babies and children.

> **Parents or carers must consider whether the clothing is:**
> - hard wearing
> - easy for the child to put on and take off
> - loose enough for movement.

A selection of clothing is necessary for night time, playtime and to suit the climate, e.g. for hot, wet and cold weather.

NIGHTWEAR

By law, children's nightwear must have a flameproof finish to the fabric so that the garment will not catch fire easily. Nightwear must be loose, comfortable and warm, with no ribbons that may get caught around the child's neck or wrists. Pyjamas are ideal for children for comfort and accessibility for the toilet. Nightdresses for girls can be cool in hot weather if made from cotton.

OUTDOOR CLOTHING

Outdoor garments need to be made from hard-wearing fabrics such as denim or corduroy. Weatherproof clothing is useful against the cold and wet weather, as are padded coats and all-in-one suits. Clothing for outdoors should be loose enough to allow movement.

PLAY CLOTHES

Play or everyday clothes should be hard wearing and easily washable – active children will easily make their clothes dirty and these will require frequent washing.

Hard-wearing play clothes

FOOTWEAR

Babies do not require footwear until they are walking. Feet need to be protected against damage and to keep them warm. However, going barefoot is very healthy for feet as it encourages them to grow strong. 'Padders' keep babies' feet cosy and offer protection when crawling.

Older children require correctly fitting shoes in order for their feet to grow and develop naturally. Children's feet can be damaged by poorly fitting

Outdoor clothing

'Padders' are suitable for babies who are not yet walking

shoes as the bones in the feet are soft and grow very quickly. A child should never be allowed to wear tight shoes or other children's shoes.

Different types of footwear

Feet should be measured every three months. Shoes should be bought from shops that offer a free fitting service and have trained fitters who offer help and advice. A wide variety of styles is available in a range of sizes, half sizes and different widths.

The process of buying shoes can be a lengthy one and shoe shops sometimes have an activity corner or an area where children can play with a selection of toys.

Parents and carers should consider the following points when choosing footwear for children:

- leather fabric is hard wearing and allows the foot to breathe
- there should be enough width and length for growth
- the shoe should offer protection and support to the foot.

Parents and carers should be aware that a child's socks and tights also need to be checked regularly to ensure that they are not too tight – this can damage the feet in the same way as tight shoes. Socks and tights should be changed as the feet grow and develop.

KEY POINTS

- Parents and carers need to be aware of the wide variety of clothing available, but to be selective when buying clothing so that whatever is chosen suits the weather and situation.
- Footwear is extremely important and should be well fitted and checked regularly to ensure that feet can grow and develop in the correct way.

KEY TASKS

1 What points should be considered when purchasing children's clothing?
2 What does the law say about children's nightwear?
3 Explain why it is important that children should wear correctly fitting shoes and socks.
4 Devise a set of guidelines, a leaflet or a poster for parents to advise them about fitting socks and shoes.
5 Suggest suitable items to provide a range of clothes for an active toddler. Indicate which items you consider to be essential and which are desirable. If you have time, you could sketch the items or collect pictures to illustrate your answer.

FURTHER WORK

Investigate the variety of children's clothing available in different outlets. Record your findings and find out the cost.

Talk about it

Thinking about clothes, does it really matter what children look like – trendy or traditional? Or is it more important that they feel warm and comfortable?

Development conditions

In order for children to grow and develop physically, certain conditions should be provided by parents and carers.

> **Babies and children need:**
> - warmth
> - routine
> - cleanliness
> - rest, exercise and fresh air
> - rest and sleep
> - good housing environment.

WARMTH

All children need to be kept warm, especially newborn babies. Older children still require warmth, but they do not require such close attention because they can maintain their own body temperature more efficiently than a newborn baby.

REST, EXERCISE AND FRESH AIR

It is important to maintain a balance of rest and exercise for children. They should be encouraged to play outside as much as possible. If the child has access to a garden, this provides a space to play. If there is no garden, regular trips to a park or play area are necessary so that the child can have the opportunity to practise physical skills such as running and climbing. Fresh air and plenty of exercise encourage the child to sleep soundly and develop a healthy appetite.

ROUTINE

A routine may be difficult to establish with a young baby, so it is often easier for a mother to fit in with the baby's natural pattern of feeding and sleeping to begin with. As the baby gets older, it is important to establish a routine for sleeping, feeding, bathing, and so on, to provide the child with a sense of security and to fit in with family life. By the age of one year the child will have some understanding of a routine.

REST AND SLEEP

It is important that a child has a regular bedtime routine, for example with a story, as this will help them to feel secure. The child may prefer a night light or the bedroom door to be left open. Many children need a comforter or favourite toy to provide a sense of security. Babies need a lot of sleep, but as the child gets older less sleep is needed. Most children have a rest or nap during the day until around the age of three, and should sleep for about 12 hours a night.

CLEANLINESS

Babies and children need to be kept clean. Babies do not need to have a daily bath – some days 'topping and tailing' will be sufficient (this is when a baby's face, hands and bottom are washed).

Bathing a baby

It is important that everything needed for bathing is collected together first so that all items are within easy reach. A baby or young child must never be left in the bath unsupervised. The water temperature should be around 37°C and should be tested with the adult's elbow or a bath thermometer to ensure it is not too hot.

> **Use the following guidelines for bathing a young baby:**
> - undress the baby (leave the nappy on for the moment) and wrap in a towel to keep it warm
> - wipe the baby's face with damp cotton wool. Do not use soap
> - wipe the eyes with a clean piece of cotton wool for each eye to prevent the spread of any infection
> - wash the baby's scalp using a mild shampoo and dry gently
> - unwrap the baby from the towel and remove the nappy, cleaning away any mess

Bathing a young baby

- gently lower the baby into the water, supporting the neck, and wash gently
- lift the baby out of the water and pat dry, being careful to dry the creases in the neck, groin, armpits and the backs of the legs.

Bathtime should be an enjoyable experience and can be built into the baby's bedtime routine if that suits the family.

Changing nappies

Ensure that this is always carried out on a flat surface and that an older baby cannot roll off. Sponge the bottom with some warm water and pat dry at each nappy change. Apply nappy cream or zinc and castor oil, as this will offer some protection against the moisture in a nappy and help prevent nappy rash.

Nappy rash

Nappy rash is caused by ammonia that is produced when urine comes into contact with bacteria (germs). This causes the skin to go red with a rash which, if left untreated, can become very sore and cause great discomfort to the baby.

To avoid nappy rash follow these guidelines:

- change the nappy frequently
- leave the nappy off if possible for some time during the day
- never leave a dirty nappy on for any length of time
- thoroughly clean the baby's skin at each nappy change by sponging with warm water
- use a nappy cream to protect the skin.

Toilet training

As with all areas of development, children learn to control their bladder and bowel at different times. The earliest age is usually around 16 months old. Bowel control is likely to be learned before bladder control and can only begin when a child starts to control the muscles that open the bladder and the bowel.

Parents and carers can help the child with toilet training by:

- not rushing the process – the child needs to be ready to co-operate and aware of having a wet or dirty nappy

- not pressurising the child into using the potty or toilet before they are ready
- providing praise and encouragement for progress
- encouraging good hygiene habits, e.g. washing hands after using the toilet.

GOOD HOUSING ENVIRONMENT

The type of housing that a child is brought up in will have an effect on their overall development. The child who lives in cramped, damp conditions in buildings that are condemned as dangerous can suffer ill health. This may lead to their progress in development being hindered or slowed down. The child's safety is also put at risk. The child needs to be brought up in a warm, safe and secure environment in order to reach his or her full potential in all areas of development.

KEY POINTS

- There are many conditions that a parent or carer should provide for their children in order for them to grow and develop.
- It is important that children have sleep, exercise and cleanliness included in their daily routine.

KEY TASKS

1. What conditions should a parent or carer provide in order for the child to grow and develop?
2. Why is it important that the child has plenty of rest, exercise and fresh air?
3. Describe briefly how to bath a baby.
4. Explain the importance of toilet training being carefully handled by the parent or carer.
5. What are the possible consequences if a baby is not given the correct conditions to develop physically?

Talk about it

Discuss the needs of babies and the importance of trying to establish a routine as soon as possible. In groups plan some daily routines for 24 hours. You could plan for the same age group or choose a different age and then compare the results.

Child safety

Accidents are the most common cause of death in children over the age of one. Children have accidents because they are not aware of the dangers in their environment. This means safety is a major responsibility for parents and carers.

ACCIDENT STATISTICS

Accident statistics show the number and types of accident that happen. Children under five are most at risk from accidents. The most serious accidents in the home happen on the stairs or in the kitchen.

The pie chart shows that falls are the cause of almost half of non-fatal accidents.

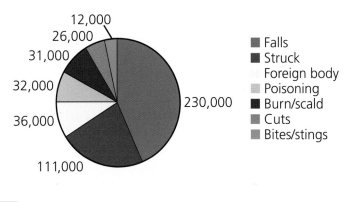

Legend:
- Falls
- Struck
- Foreign body
- Poisoning
- Burn/scald
- Cuts
- Bites/stings

12,000
26,000
31,000
32,000
36,000
111,000
230,000

Non-fatal accidents in the home to children under five years of age
Source: RoSPA

These statistics are for accidents where children are injured, but more than 100 young children die every year from fatal accidents in the home. House fires are the most common cause of accidental death in the home to children under five.

FOR FURTHER REFERENCE The Royal Society for the Prevention of Accidents (RoSPA) is a charitable organisation that provides an information service to promote home safety and prevent accidents. Visit its website via our hotlinks website.

SAFETY AND DEVELOPMENTAL STAGES

Babies and children are more at risk from particular hazards at different stages in their development. A hazard is a potential danger, such as a hot drink or a sharp edge on a toy.

Newborn babies should never be left alone on raised surfaces as they could roll over and fall off.

Six-month-old babies put anything in their mouths that they can grasp. As soon as babies start to move about and explore, the chance of accidents increases.

Toddlers learn to develop their skills of locomotion. They try to balance and climb up on objects.

Three-year-olds are adventurous and want to explore and test their skills.

Four-year-olds are more independent and keen to try activities such as riding a bike or swinging on a rope.

Dangers can be explained to a two-year-old

Fewer accidents happen when children are supervised

PARENTS AND CARERS

Parents and carers need to be aware of the potential dangers for their child at different stages of development. When the child is ready, adults need to make them aware of these dangers. Very young children cannot understand danger. It is not until the age of about two years that a child starts to understand how some actions have consequences, such as if they touch a hot iron it will hurt. Helping children to learn about the dangers around them without stopping their natural curiosity and growing independence is a difficult balance to achieve.

WHY CHILDREN HAVE ACCIDENTS

Children have accidents for a number of reasons.

Children may have accidents because:

- they are often absorbed in activities and unaware of the danger in their surroundings
- they lack experience and do not understand the consequences of what they do
- they are naturally curious and inquisitive – this can often lead them into danger
- they are small and often cannot see the hazards around them which are obvious to adults
- they are overexcited or emotionally upset.

Other risk factors include:

- supervision – many accidents happen when children are not supervised
- time of day – more accidents happen in the late afternoon or evening, in the summer or at weekends
- gender – boys are more likely to have accidents than girls
- emotional factors and stress such as illness or death in the family increase the likelihood of having an accident.

KEY TASKS

1 Explain the reasons why children under five have more accidents than older children.
2 Describe how parents and carers can help their children to be aware of potential hazards.
3 Explain why babies and young children are more at risk from particular hazards at different stages in their development.
4 Create a chart to show which accidents may possibly happen to children at different ages and stages.

Talk about it

Discuss the key points that parents need to be made aware of to help prevent them putting their children in danger. Use the information to create a PowerPoint presentation that could be used in the parents' waiting area at nursery.

Accident prevention

Accidents can be prevented. No home or garden can be made totally accident-proof, but an awareness of likely hazards reduces the risk of accidents.

CREATING A SAFE ENVIRONMENT FOR CHILDREN

Hazards can be identified and action can be taken to prevent accidents in the home. Serious accidents often happen in the kitchen.

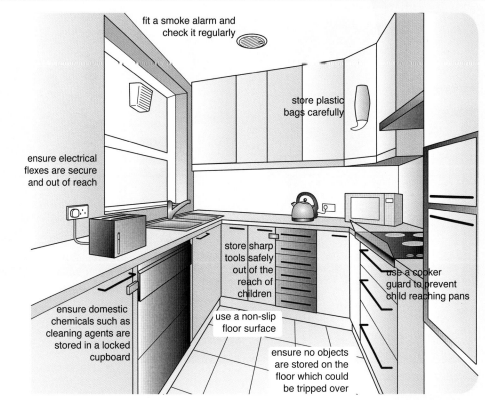

fit a smoke alarm and check it regularly

store plastic bags carefully

ensure electrical flexes are secure and out of reach

store sharp tools safely out of the reach of children

use a cooker guard to prevent child reaching pans

use a non-slip floor surface

ensure domestic chemicals such as cleaning agents are stored in a locked cupboard

ensure no objects are stored on the floor which could be tripped over

Actions that can be taken to make a kitchen area safe

Accident prevention in the home

Accidental injury	Hazard	Prevention
Falls	Falling down stairs and steps, rolling off surfaces, falling out of cots/prams/buggies, falling out of windows	Use of safety gates and window locks, ensure stair area is well lit, teach safe way to climb stairs, supervision of activity sessions
Choking and suffocation	Objects put in mouth, choking on food, suffocation by plastic bags	Always supervise a young child when they are eating, keep small objects such as buttons out of reach, store plastic bags safely
Cuts	Sharp tools left out, broken glass, sharp edges to objects in the home	Keep sharp tools out of reach, use safety glass or safety (shatter-resistant) film on vulnerable doors such as patio doors
Electrocution	Poking objects into plug sockets, handling electrical equipment, unsafe electrical equipment	Use socket guards, regularly check safety of electrical equipment, teach children dangers of electricity when they are old enough to understand
Scalds and burns	Hot surfaces in the kitchen, hot liquids in kettles, fires, hot water in bath	Supervise children closely in kitchen area, take particular care with hot drinks, use cooker guards and fireguards, test temperature of bath water
Poisoning	Household chemicals such as bleach, tablets and medications, alcohol accessible to child	Keep all household chemicals in original, labelled container, securely stored, keep medicines stored in a locked cabinet, store alcohol safely out of reach
Drowning	Child left alone in bath, uncovered bowls or buckets of liquid in the home, unsupervised access to paddling pools and ponds	Children must always be supervised as they can drown in just a few centimetres of water

FIRST AID

All small children have minor accidents as they grow up, so it is important for homes to have a basic first aid box that parents or carers can use.

HAZARDOUS SUBSTANCES

Every year almost 10 000 children are rushed to hospital because they have swallowed a hazardous substance. Most of these hazardous substances are common household chemicals such as bleach, anti-freeze, aftershave or toilet cleaner. Children under the age of five are naturally curious, and like investigating brightly coloured and unusually shaped containers. Hazardous substances are labelled clearly to show parents and carers the dangers

Warning labels on hazardous household chemicals

Label	Description of substance
Harmful/irritant	A substance that is not a serious health risk but may cause ill health if it is inhaled, swallowed or spilt on the skin. Some of these substances may irritate the eyes and skin
Toxic/very toxic	Can cause serious risk to health if swallowed and in some cases if inhaled or spilt on the skin
Corrosive	May cause painful burns and destroys body tissue

REDUCING THE RISKS

It is possible to do certain things to reduce the risks of accidents to children.

The risks can be reduced as follows:

- over half of the accidental poisonings happen when children are left on their own for less than five minutes – young children should not be left unsupervised
- children are attracted by the colour and shape of containers – keep all household chemicals out of sight and out of reach of children
- many of the accidents with household chemicals happen to children under three years of age – remember that children of this age cannot understand the dangers

- accidents can happen if hazardous substances are stored in a different container – always store products in their original containers

KEY POINTS

- An awareness of the most likely hazards can reduce the risk of accidents.
- Young children should never be left unsupervised.
- Serious accidents often happen in the kitchen.
- All homes should have a basic first aid box for parents or carers to use.
- Many household chemicals are hazardous.
- All household chemicals should be kept out of sight and out of reach of children.

KEY TASKS

1 Look at the actions that can be taken to make the kitchen safer. Identify each of the hazards and explain the type of accidental injury that would be caused if the action was not taken.

2 Choose a room where toddlers play and identify the possible safety hazards. Suggest actions that could be taken to prevent accidents. Display the information you have gathered in a table:

Hazard identified	Action to be taken

FURTHER WORK

Design a poster – which could be used in your local health centre – to show the dangers of some common household substances.

GradeStudio

When you read exam questions like those below:

Remember: 1a says **items** and 1b says **ways**.

1a Name 2 items of safety equipment that parents or carers could buy to help prevent accidents to toddlers in the home. (2 marks)

1b Suggest 3 ways in which parents or carers could protect children from the dangers of swallowing a poisonous household substance or chemical. (3 marks)

Safety outside the home

PLAYING OUTSIDE

The garden is seen as a safe place for children to play, but there are a number of hazards that exist. Young children should be supervised when they are playing outside in the garden.

Hazards in the garden may include:

- poisonous plants such as laburnum
- bacteria from animal faeces
- water (children can drown in a few centimetres)
- rusty and broken objects
- access to roads through broken fences.

Play equipment

Play and adventure areas are exciting places for children under the age of five to explore. They are designed with safety in mind. The British Standard for play equipment is BS 5696 and regulation relating to playground equipment is complex.

Key safety points include the following:

- all swings should have rubber seats to soften the impact if they hit a child
- swings for younger children should have cradle seats
- slides should be set in slopes or banks
- floor areas should be made of materials that cushion falls, such as bark chippings
- there should be plenty of space between play equipment and play areas should be fenced off.

Play equipment helps children to develop their physical skills

Adventure playgrounds can help children to develop their physical skills and their independence as they are encouraged to test themselves in activities. They are appropriate for children of the right age, but parents and carers have to decide at what age a child is ready to try out his or her skills.

ROAD SAFETY

The number of children under five killed or seriously injured in accidents when playing in or near roads has fallen in recent years. However, in the UK these figures are still higher than in the rest of Europe. Different government campaigns have aimed to reduce the number of children being killed or injured on or near roads.

Young children are particularly at risk because:

- they do not understand the dangers
- they cannot judge the speed or distance of traffic
- their size makes it difficult for them to have a good view of traffic.

The Green Cross Code

This is a system designed to help children understand how to cross the road safely in today's traffic. The code teaches the child to follow a simple procedure to cross the road safely. Children under five years should never be out alone and should learn safety rules by example every time they are out with adults. Children aged five or under cannot assess the speed of cars or understand the danger.

Children learn by example

Children aged five may learn the Green Cross Code, but may not understand it. They should not be expected to follow the code on their own. It is only when the child is older, at about seven years of age, that he or she will be able to follow and understand the rules of the Green Cross Code.

Let's Decide Walk Wise

The Let's Decide Walk Wise project has been introduced as part of a road safety campaign designed to create a better awareness of road safety and to reduce the number of children killed or injured in road accidents.

TRAVELLING SAFELY BY CAR

The law states that all children who travel in a car must be in a **safety restraint** up to the age of 12 years or 135 cm in height. Injuries to children in car accidents can be reduced by wearing a suitable child restraint or seat belt. There are a wide variety of child restraints depending on the weight, size and age of the child. They are categorised by weight and age to help parents and carers choose the most appropriate seat. It is essential that the car seats and restraints are fitted correctly and that the harnesses and straps are adjusted before each journey. All child seats and restraints must carry a **British Standards kitemark**.

Types of restraint

Rear-facing baby seats can also be used to carry babies outside the car. Head huggers are often supplied to support the heads of newborn babies. These carriers are only suitable for babies up to about 9 months old and weighing less than 13 kg. They can be used in the front or the back of the car. However, it is illegal to use a rear-facing baby seat in the front if the car has air bags fitted.

Forward-facing child safety seats fit in the front or back of the car. They are suitable for children from nine months to four years weighing 9–18 kg. The choice depends on the child's size and weight.

Booster seats are designed to hold the child securely and comfortably between the ages of approximately four to six years (up to 15 kg).

Booster cushions allow the older child aged from six to 11 years (up to 22 kg) to be raised high enough to see out of the window while holding them securely in the adult seat belt.

KEY POINTS

- Gardens can contain many hazards for young children.
- The Green Cross Code is a system to help children understand how to cross the road safely.
- All children who travel in a car must be in a safety restraint.
- All child restraints must carry a British Standards kitemark.

KEY TASKS

1 Explain why young children have so many road accidents.
2 Design an informative poster to help a five-year-old child understand the Green Cross Code.
3 Write an article for your local paper to create an awareness of safety in your local area.

FURTHER WORK

Investigation: visit a children's play area and assess whether it is a safe place for children to play, giving your reasons.

Think about it

How can you set a good example when crossing the road?

Safety issues

CHILD-RELATED PRODUCTS

It is essential that products which are used with children are safe. Consumer law such as the General Product Safety Regulations (2005) makes sure that manufacturers of products comply with the standards set down by the government. Some products where safety is an important factor, such as pushchairs, also have to conform to a British Standard.

The British Standards kitemark

British Standards kitemark

The kitemark of the British Standards Institute is found on a wide range of products and equipment used by children such as safety gates, car seats, pushchairs and electrical equipment. The British Standards Institute checks the product against an agreed standard to make sure it will perform its job properly and safely. Its tests judge the quality and suitability of the materials the product is made out of, as well as the safety and design features of the product.

TOY SAFETY

Playing with toys is an essential part of every child's development, but toys are involved in about 30 000 accidents every year. A safe toy is one that does not harm the child in any way. Toys are designed for a specific age of child to match their stage of development. Toys used by children at the wrong age could cause a hazard. For example, a nine-month-old baby playing with small plastic dice could swallow and choke on the dice. Toys should be kept in a clean condition, particularly those for young babies who put everything in their mouths. Toys should be checked regularly to make sure they have no loose parts and no sharp edges to harm a child.

Toys and the law

The Toys (Safety) Regulations (1995) make sure that toys which are sold in the UK are safe. To comply with the law, toys are tested in many ways. For example, there is a test to check that the materials the toys are made out of are safe. Textiles used to make toys, both in the outside construction and the filling, should be non-flammable. Plastics, metals and paints used must be non-toxic. When buying toys for children, look for the following symbols on the product:

The CE Mark shows that the toy meets the standards of the European Toy Safety Directive

The Lion Mark is found on toys made in the UK and shows that the toy meets the safety requirements of the British Toy and Hobby Association

SAFETY OF CHILDREN'S NIGHTWEAR

The Nightwear (Safety) Regulations state that all children's nightwear must pass a test for slow-burning fabrics. Any children's clothes made from terry towelling, which can be very flammable, must carry a permanent label to show whether the clothes have passed the low flammability test.

LOW FLAMMABILITY TO BS 5722	KEEP AWAY FROM FIRE

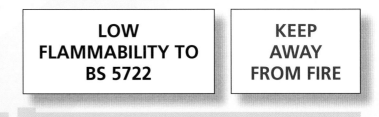

THE TOY SAFETY CODE
* Buy a safe toy
* Buy toys for the right age
* Throw away broken toys
* Keep toys tidy

The toy safety code   *Clothing safety*

If the 'keep away from fire' label is on an item of children's clothing, extreme care is needed as the fabric the clothes are made from is not slow burning.

Many children's clothes are bought by mail order – the labels for mail order clothes may look different but mean exactly the same thing.

If parents and carers make nightwear for children themselves, they should choose a low flammability fabric, threads and trimmings.

PERSONAL SAFETY

National campaigns to promote the personal safety of children, such as the 'Say no' campaign, have raised the awareness of the community about child safety. Safety has become more of an issue today as many parents and carers spend time away from their children while at work and entrust their care to others.

Parents and carers today worry about their children being abducted. This happens very rarely, but it is sensible for young children to be given simple guidelines about how to cope if they should ever find themselves on their own.

Safety guidelines for children could include:
- never going with anyone they do not know
- letting their parents or carers know if they are approached by anyone
- if lost, wait and stand still until they are found.

THE EFFECTS OF DIVERSE FAMILY LIFESTYLES

Family lifestyles have changed a lot in recent years and have become a lot more diverse. For example, in many families both parents are working which means older children may spend some time in the home unsupervised before the parents return from work. If a child is hungry or thirsty, it may try to cook something or make a hot drink. If a child is cold, it might start a fire. Parents should discuss the possible hazards with their children and put measures in place to prevent accidents happening.

SUMMARY OF CHILD SAFETY

All children tend to have accidents despite the best intentions of parents and carers to prevent them. Young children cannot concentrate on more than one thing at a time – if a child is playing with a ball which rolls into the road they will think about chasing

the ball not the danger of the road. Children need to explore as part of their growing independence and parents and carers need to allow children this opportunity but in a safe, supervised environment.

Some things can be done to help prevent accidents:
- parents and carers need to be aware of safety hazards
- parents and carers should take action to improve the safety of the child's environment
- young children must be adequately supervised
- adults must show good examples of appropriate behaviour
- the design and labelling of products related to child safety should be improved.

KEY TASKS

1 **Describe the safety points that are important when choosing toys for children.**

2 **Explain why young children are more likely to have accidents than older children.**

3 **How does the British Standards Institute test products to make sure they are safe?**

4 **Explain why it is important to protect children from dangerous toys.**

FURTHER WORK

Carry out a survey of toys or nightwear for a young baby to find out if the products are correctly labelled.

Talk about it

Are children really any more at risk these days than in the past?

In groups, debate this point. Give feedback to others.

GradeStudio

You might get an exam question like this:

Give four safety points that someone buying a toy for a four-year-old child should look for. (4 marks)

Remember: Do not include 'don't get a toy with small parts that the child could put into their mouth' as the question relates to a four-year-old and such information relates to children who are younger than three years.

ExamCafé
Unit 3

3 months
has some head control
follows objects with eyes
responds to name
plays with hands

6 months
good head control
sits up with support
reaches for objects
turns towards sounds

9 months
crawls
uses pincer grasp
can stand with support

12 months
recognises people and sounds
points at objects
walks with support

18 months
walks steadily
recognises own reflection
can hold a pencil

2–3 years
uses tripod and pincer grasp
starting to use preferred hand
rides push-along toy
recognises itself in photos

> I could never remember what children should be able to do at each stage so I started to make myself a chart to revise from.
>
> Ayesha

You can do one for yourself or you could finish this one.

> I can't remember long-winded notes so I like to summarise things in a spidergram, like this.
>
> Bobby

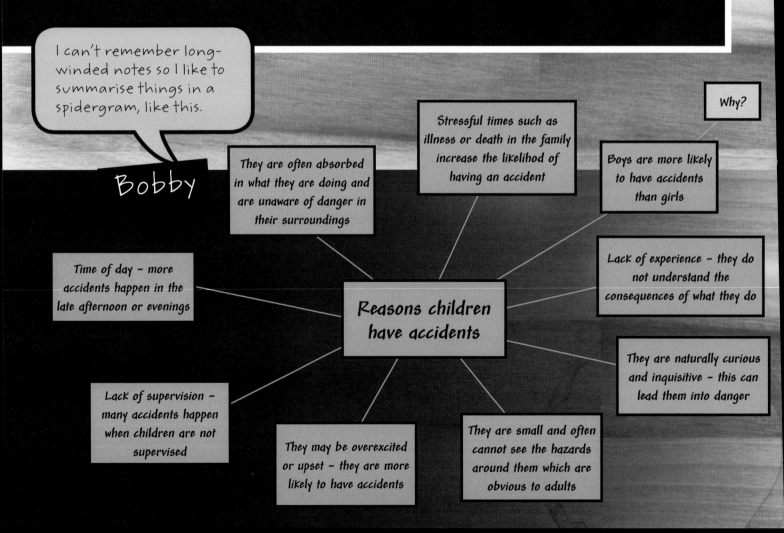

Reasons children have accidents

- They are often absorbed in what they are doing and are unaware of danger in their surroundings
- Stressful times such as illness or death in the family increase the likelihod of having an accident
- Why?
- Boys are more likely to have accidents than girls
- Lack of experience – they do not understand the consequences of what they do
- They are naturally curious and inquisitive – this can lead them into danger
- They are small and often cannot see the hazards around them which are obvious to adults
- They may be overexcited or upset – they are more likely to have accidents
- Lack of supervision – many accidents happen when children are not supervised
- Time of day – more accidents happen in the late afternoon or evenings

74

Revision checklist

Things I really need to remember…

Unit 3 revision checklist: characteristics and reflex actions of newborns		
Physical characteristics	fontanelle	❑
	umbilical cord	❑
	hair	❑
	shape	❑
	weight	❑
	length	❑
	head circumference	❑
Reflex actions	sucking	❑
	rooting	❑
	stepping	❑
	falling/'Moro'	❑
	grasp	❑
	startle	❑
Skin	vernix	❑
	lanugo	❑

Common mistakes

Be careful with some words which may sound similar but mean very different things!

Think about which word you are using – have you chosen the correct term?

- Flammable/inflammable means something will catch fire
- Non-flammable/unflammable/flameproof means something will not catch fire!

Be very careful to **say what you really mean!**

ExamCafé

Exam preparation

Below are some examples of answers that are too brief to explain what the writer is trying to say.

Unit 3 sample exam question:
Give three things to look for when choosing shoes for a three-year-old child. **(3 marks)**

Student answer

1 Size
2 Shape
3 Colour

Why not?
There's nothing wrong with that answer!

Examiner says:
There are no marks at all for this answer.

Examiner tips:

Instead of just saying *size* – which doesn't tell us anything – the student should have put:

• 'The shoes must be the correct size, length and width to fit the child's feet.'

Instead of saying *shape* (a circle or square is a shape!) the student should have put:

• 'The shoes should be of a suitable shape with a rounded end at the toe to allow room for the child's toes to move.'

The word *colour* does not explain what the student means. The student could have put:

• 'Choose a shoe which is the child's favourite colour to encourage them to wear the shoes.'

Always be wary of writing single word answers like this. Can one word really explain what you are trying to say?

Here is another example of the same problem.

Unit 3 sample exam question:
Suggest three things a parent/carer could look for when buying nightwear for a three-year-old child. **(3 marks)**

Student answer

1 Material
2 Comfortable
3 Flammable

Examiner says:
Again, there are no marks at all for this answer!

Examiner tips:

- All nightwear is made of material but the student has not given the right answer – 'a soft fabric which is cool in summer, warm in winter.'
- Comfortable – does that mean stretchy to allow the child the comfort to move around in bed?
- Flammable – oh dear! Flammable means 'will catch fire easily' and is **definitely not** what the student meant.

Key words	
bonding	the unconditional love developed between parents and their child
British Standards kitemark	a symbol that indicates that a product has been tested to given standards
cot death	the sudden, unexplained death of a baby
developmental screening tests	tests that are carried out regularly to assess a child's development
fine manipulative skills	the precise use of the hands and fingers
fontanelle	the soft spot on top of a newborn baby's head
gross motor skills	the use of the large muscles of the body
hand–eye co-ordination	the ability to connect the movement of the hands with what the eyes can see
incubator	a piece of equipment that supports and protects an underdeveloped newborn baby
jaundice	a condition due to the immaturity of a newborn baby's liver, which causes the skin and eyes to be tinged yellow
low birth-weight babies	babies that weigh less than 2.5 kg (5.5 lb) at birth
milestones	a way of assessing the progress of a child's development
premature babies	babies born before week 37 of pregnancy
reflex actions	automatic movements caused by a newborn baby's senses being stimulated
safety restraint	a device to keep a child safe while travelling
vernix	a greasy coating on a newborn baby's skin

Exam tips

- Highlight the main points in the question.
- Make sure you know how many points you need to include by looking at the mark (in brackets) at the end of the question: 1 mark = at least 1 good point.
- If the question says 'describe' make sure that you do just that – use a full description in your answer.

Feeding the newborn baby

BREASTFEEDING

Food is a basic need for a newborn baby. Babies are born with a natural reflex to suck. If a baby is put to its mother's breast after birth, it will start to suck. The first milk from the mother's breast is **colostrum**. This is a protein-rich liquid that contains antibodies from the mother to protect the baby from infection. The colostrum is produced for two or three days after the birth, after which the breast starts to produce milk (lactate).

Breastfeeding the newborn baby

NUTRITIONAL REQUIREMENTS OF A NEWBORN BABY

Breast milk can supply all the nutrients a baby needs. Breast milk differs in composition from cows' milk, which is not suitable for babies. This is because it contains different proportions of the nutrients. **Formula milk** is the name given to manufactured milks and milk powders designed for babies. It is the only alternative to breast milk for babies up to the age of six months. Formula milks are modified to make sure they contain the correct nutritional balance for a baby. Different formula milks are available to suit the stages of feeding.

CHOICE OF MILK

Cows' milk is not suitable for young babies as it has more protein and salt (sodium) than breast milk.

The nutritional value of different milks per 100 g

Nutrient	Breast	Formula	Cows'
Protein (g)	1.2	1.5	3.3
Fat (g)	3.8	3.6	3.7
Carbohydrate (g)	7.0	7.2	4.8
Sodium (mg)	15	15	58
Calcium (mg)	125	44	44
Phosphorus (mg)	15	30	96
Iron (mg)	0.08	0.12	0.10
Vitamin A (µg)	58	79	40
Vitamin C (µg)	4.3	5.6	1.6
Vitamin D (µg)	0.01	1.1	1.6

High levels of sodium can be harmful to a baby and can cause kidney damage. One of the proteins in milk is called casein and cows' milk has a higher proportion of casein, which babies find difficult to digest. Cows' milk should not be given until the baby is a year old. Formula milk is usually made from cows' milk, but it has been modified to contain less casein and make it suitable for babies. Formula milk is similar in nutritional value to breast milk.

THE CHOICE OF FEEDING METHOD

The mother will have made the decision whether to breast or bottle feed during pregnancy. There are many factors that may affect the decision she makes. Sometimes the decision will be made for practical reasons such as the mother's return to work.

Many mothers will use both methods of feeding, starting with breastfeeding and moving on to bottle feeding or using bottle feeding to supplement the breastfeeds.

Formula milk products

Some factors that may affect the decision about the choice of feeding method include:

- cost
- mother's employment pattern
- parents' or carers' lifestyles
- personal viewpoint of parents
- cultural background.

THE NURSING MOTHER

Breastfeeding is considered to be the best method for feeding because breast milk is ideally suited to the baby. A breastfeeding mother is often called a nursing mother or is said to be lactating because she is feeding milk to the baby. The production of milk in the breasts is triggered by the birth of the baby.

Nursing mothers should make sure their diet contains calcium-rich foods and plenty of fluid. Substances taken by the nursing mother are absorbed into her body and passed to the feeding baby, so alcohol and medicines should be avoided whenever possible.

Advantages of breastfeeding are that:

- it is free and convenient
- it helps the development of a bond between mother and baby as they spend a lot of time in close physical contact with each other
- it helps the mother's uterus return to shape after pregnancy as it stimulates the hormone that controls this
- it uses up 1300 kilocalories a day, which helps the mother to return to her previous weight.

Feeding routines

Breastfed babies are often fed on demand – that is to say, when they are hungry. This means many feeds when the baby is new, perhaps up to ten a day. However, after the first few weeks the baby will settle down to a regular pattern of feeding. This will mean about six feeds in 24 hours, depending on the birth weight of the baby. Low birth-weight babies need smaller feeds. Gradually the intervals between the feeds get longer, until at about three months the baby no longer needs a night feed.

Breast milk is the perfect food for babies because:

- it provides the correct amount of nutrients for the baby
- it is easier for the baby to digest
- it contains antibodies to protect the baby from infections
- breastfed babies have less chance of having gastroenteritis than bottle-fed babies
- it helps reduce the risks of allergies and diseases such as eczema in young children
- it is a convenient way of feeding the baby – milk is always at the right temperature, is clean and available.

KEY POINTS

- **Babies are born with a natural reflex to suck.**
- **Breast milk supplies all the nutrients a baby requires.**
- **Formula milks are modified to make sure they contain the right amounts of nutrients for babies.**
- **A range of factors affect the decision whether or not to breastfeed.**
- **Breastfeeding offers the best start in life for a baby, so it makes sense to try it.**

KEY TASKS

1 **What is the function of colostrum?**
2 **Explain why cows' milk is unsuitable for the newborn baby.**
3 **Explain the factors that influence the mother's choice of feeding method.**
4 **Research breastfeeding to find out as many reasons as possible to show why it is strongly recommended as the best possible start for the baby.**

FURTHER WORK

Carry out a survey to find out about attitudes to breastfeeding or choices of feeding method. Present your findings in a short report.

Think about it

There are advantages and disadvantages to breast and bottle feeding. Which would you choose and why?

Bottle feeding

Some mothers choose to bottle feed their babies. If the baby is correctly bottle-fed there is no reason why they should not thrive and develop in the same way as a breastfed baby.

There is a wide range of infant formula milks on the market, all modified to provide the correct nutrients for a baby. Products are designed for babies of various ages, with the proportions of the different nutrients modified according to the age of the baby.

 LINK For more information on formula milk see pages 78–79.

Parents and carers need to be able to calculate the correct amount of feed for their baby. Calculation charts can be found on all formula milk products.

FORMULA MILKS

Most formula milks are in powder form and need making up into a feed. Instructions on how to do this are given on the formula milk product. It is very important that the instructions are followed. If too much formula milk powder is used to make up the feed the nutrients will be too concentrated. This can cause the baby to put on too much weight. It could also cause more serious side effects, such as loss of consciousness, as the baby will be getting too high a level of sodium. Some formula milks are in liquid form and are ready to use.

FEEDING BOTTLES

A wide variety of feeding bottles are available, which have been designed for ease of use.

> **Well-designed feeding bottles have:**
> - a wide neck for easy cleaning
> - graduated measures on the side, which are easy to read
> - a special cap to keep the teat clean
> - clear plastic so you can see that it is clean.

Making up a formula milk feed

1 Wash hands before starting and ensure all equipment has been washed and sterilised.

3 Pour cooled boiled water into the feeding bottle up to the appropriate measure level.

2 Boil water for feed and allow it to cool down.

4 Using a sterilised knife to level the powder, add the correct number of scoops of formula milk into the bottle.

5 Place the cap on the feeding bottle and shake to dissolve the milk powder.

6 Cool the milk to the correct temperature (approximately 37°C).

7 Test the temperature of the milk on the inside of the wrist before use.

STERILISING FEEDING EQUIPMENT

For the baby's first year, all feeding equipment should be sterilised to prevent bacteria spreading

Sterilising equipment is essential during the baby's first year

an infection to the baby. The sterilising process is usually carried out using chemical, microwave or electric steam sterilising equipment. The instructions for sterilising the equipment must be followed carefully. All the equipment used when preparing feeds, including any brushes that are used to clean the teats and bottles, should be sterilised.

HOW TO BOTTLE FEED A BABY

The guidelines below advise on how to bottle feed a baby.

When bottle feeding:

- prepare the feed and warm the bottle if necessary by standing it in some hot water
- check that the teat hole is not blocked
- hold the baby in a comfortable position and place the teat in the baby's mouth
- make sure the bottle is tilted so that the teat is always full of milk, otherwise the baby will take in air which can give it wind.
- let the baby feed at its own pace
- the baby may need to bring up wind during the feed – one way of doing this is by holding the baby against a shoulder and rubbing its back gently
- at the end of the feed, throw away any milk that is left.

A feeding pattern for the bottle-fed baby will develop in a similar way to that of the breastfed baby. Some bottle-fed babies are fed on schedule, which means at regular times rather than when the baby feels hungry. A close bond with the parents and carers who feed the baby will build up.

Some young babies have been left with a bottle propped up against a pillow – sometimes called prop feeding. This is a dangerous practice as a young baby could choke.

Advantages of bottle feeding are that:

- the adult can see exactly how much milk the baby is taking
- other people besides the mother can feed the baby and build up a bond with the baby
- babies can be fed anywhere without possible embarrassment
- it is less tiring for some mothers than breastfeeding.

KEY POINTS

- **Choose the correct type of formula milk for the age of the baby.**
- **Accurately measure the correct amount of feed.**
- **Make sure all feeding equipment is thoroughly washed and sterilised.**
- **When feeding the baby, hold the bottle at the correct angle to prevent wind.**

KEY TASKS

1 Explain the advantages of bottle feeding for a mother who is going back to work after her baby is born.
2 Prepare an instruction sheet to describe how to make up a bottle feed for a two-month-old baby.
3 Why is it important to follow the instructions carefully when sterilising feeding equipment?
4 Consider the alternative methods and then make your recommendations to a new mum about her choice of sterilising equipment. Give clear reasons for your suggestions.

FURTHER WORK

1 Carry out research to find out the range of different formula milk products that are available and their cost. Present your findings to your group.
2 Find out the cost of a formula milk product. Calculate the cost of feeding a two-week-old baby for a week. Present your findings.

Bottle feeding means dads can also feed their babies

Mixed feeding

Milk provides all the food a baby needs for at least the first six months of life. As babies gain weight and grow older, they need a more varied diet. The changeover from milk to more solid food is called **weaning** or mixed feeding.

> **A baby may be ready to start weaning when it:**
> - appears restless or hungry after a feed
> - starts waking at night when it has previously slept through
> - appears to want to be fed more often.

When a baby first starts to be weaned, milk will continue to provide most of the nutrients it needs. As the baby grows older, solid food will gradually become a more important part of its diet and the amount of milk given can be reduced. Weaning is a gradual process, with new foods being introduced slowly, one at a time.

STAGES OF WEANING

There are three main stages to go through in the weaning process.

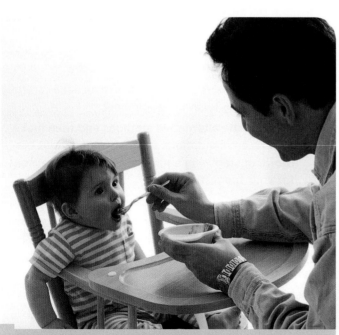
Babies are introduced to new foods gradually

Stage 1
Young babies cannot chew and the first weaning foods need to be of a similar consistency to milk. Baby cereal, such as rice mixed with formula milk, is a suitable first weaning food. The food can be given on a spoon and should be at the same temperature as their usual milk feed. Vegetable and fruit purées made to the same smooth consistency are also suitable foods.

Stage 2
As babies get used to spoon-feeding they will take more solid food. They can begin to have the same food as the rest of the family, mashed or puréed. Babies are able to chew at this stage so can be given some hard foods to chew. These are called finger foods and include items such as rusks and slices of peeled apple. Babies will start to pick up food to put in their mouths. To avoid the risk of choking, do not leave babies unattended while eating.

Stage 3
By the age of nine months to one year, the baby will probably be eating solid foods with a top-up milk drink from a feeder cup. A wide variety of foods should be given with a range of textures, because the baby can now cope with food that is lumpier in texture.

FOOD PRODUCTS FOR WEANING

Weaning foods can be easily and simply prepared at home by sieving, liquidising or mashing foods. Food prepared for weaning the baby should not have extra salt or sugar added. The flavour of the food itself is enough for a baby – flavours that are too strong at this stage may affect the baby's sense of taste for different foods.

A wide range of food products suitable for weaning babies at different stages is available in supermarkets. They vary from dehydrated products, such as baby rice, to jars, packets, tins and cartons of all types of foods. There are strict controls to limit any additional sugar, salt or additives. Prepared food products for weaning are sold in tamper-proof or tamper-evident packaging to ensure the hygienic quality of the food product.

Ideal foods to start weaning are:

- mashed vegetables, e.g. carrot
- mashed fruit, e.g. banana
- gluten-free cereal products, e.g. baby rice.

Foods to progress to include:

- custard
- fromage frais
- different fruits and vegetables
- yoghurt
- other mashed foods that are not too spicy.

Most parents and carers use some prepared baby food products as part of their child's diet

Prepared food products for weaning

There are advantages and disadvantages to using ready-made baby foods.

Advantages of prepared weaning products:

- a wide range of foods are available
- easy and quick to use
- the nutritional content is stated on the packet
- some products have added nutrients

- the product is safe to eat as it is hygienically prepared and packed
- products are particularly useful when travelling.

Disadvantages of prepared weaning products:

- more expensive than home-made products
- there may be some wastage if only a small quantity is required
- some additives are present in some products
- it is not always possible to tell the amount and proportion of nutrients in all the products.

KEY POINTS

- Babies need to go at their own pace when learning about new tastes and textures.
- Babies like to feed themselves, which is messy, but it is a stage they need to experience.
- Babies know when they have eaten enough so they should not be forced to eat more.
- It is important to take as much care with food hygiene when preparing weaning foods for a baby as when preparing milk feeds.

KEY TASKS

1 What signs show a baby is ready to start weaning?
2 Explain the stages of weaning.
3 Why should sugar and salt not be added to a baby's food?
4 It is important to make sure that the child has a wide variety of nutritious foods right from the start of weaning. Explain why this should be the case.

FURTHER WORK

1 Carry out a survey of weaning foods at your local supermarket. Identify the range of products available for each stage of weaning. Present your findings.
2 Compare the cost, quality and convenience of home-made and prepared weaning foods. Present your results.

Think about it (for homework)

Have you ever looked at a baby food label? What does baby food contain?

Nutrition (1)

NUTRIENTS

Nutrition is a study of the nutrients found in the foods in our diet. An understanding of nutrition is important when providing healthy meals for babies and young children.

The function of nutrients is to:

- help the body grow and repair
- provide energy in order to carry out physical activity
- keep the body warm
- help carry out other essential processes such as digestion.

Foods usually contain more than one nutrient. For example, milk contains protein, fat, carbohydrate, vitamins and minerals.

MACRONUTRIENTS

The word **macronutrient** refers to nutrients that the body needs in large amounts. Proteins, carbohydrates and fats are macronutrients.

PROTEIN

Protein is needed for the growth and repair of body tissues such as the blood cells and muscles. Babies and young children grow rapidly and the protein needs of a child are high. Protein-rich foods come from both animal and vegetable sources. Some high-protein foods are expensive and cheaper sources can be just as nutritious.

Protein comes from animal and plant sources

Protein complementation

Proteins are made up of smaller units called **amino acids** and there are many different types. For a protein to be of use to the body to grow new tissue, the right amount and proportion needs to be eaten.

Animal protein sources contain all the amino acids needed to build tissue, known as the indispensable amino acids. These animal sources of protein are referred to as of high biological value (HBV).

Vegetable protein sources, such as cereals and pulses, contain some but not all of the indispensable amino acids. They are referred to as of low biological value (LBV).

If two different vegetable sources of protein are eaten together in a meal, such as a pulse (beans) with a cereal (toast), all the indispensable amino acids will be present and the meal will be of high biological value.

Combining sources of protein in this way is called protein complementation and is particularly important for babies and young children on a vegetarian diet.

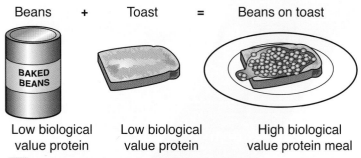

| Beans | + | Toast | = | Beans on toast |

Low biological value protein   Low biological value protein   High biological value protein meal

The complementation of proteins

CARBOHYDRATES

Carbohydrate foods provide the body with energy.

Types of carbohydrates are:

- sugars, which are found in fruits, cakes, biscuits and soft drinks
- starches, such as potatoes, bread, pasta and rice.

Sugar contains only empty calories and should be eaten in moderation

Sugars

Sugar is added to many foods during their manufacture or during the preparation of food in the home. In fruit and some vegetables sugar is found in the form of glucose and fructose, while in cereals it is found as maltose and in milk as lactose.

The amount of sugary food eaten should be limited, as sugar provides only 'empty calories' and encourages children to have a 'sweet tooth'. Sugar should not be added to the drinks given to children.

Starches

Starches are good sources of energy because, unlike sugar, they are found with other nutrients. For example, starches are found in bread, which also contains proteins, vitamins, minerals and dietary fibre, so it is a healthier option. Starches have always been a mainstay of children's diet in the UK and they are often referred to as staple foods.

When starch sources such as wheat and rice are processed, they lose some of their nutrients and dietary fibre. Less processed starch products, such as wholewheat flour, bread and pasta, are therefore more nutritious.

DIETARY FIBRE

Dietary fibre is a form of carbohydrate which is not used for energy. It is also called non-starch polysaccharide (NSP) or cellulose. It is found in raw plant material, in the outer coating of cereals and in the structure of fruit and vegetables – it is the tough fibrous part of plants. The body cannot digest dietary fibre so it passes through the body, absorbing water and increasing in bulk. This helps stimulate the digestive system to work properly and to avoid constipation.

FATS

Fats are the most concentrated form of energy. They are found in food products such as butter, oil and cream. Fats are also present in other foods such as cheese, cakes and chocolate, and in fried foods such as chips, where they are referred to as invisible fats.

Although fats are a useful source of energy, too much can be harmful because of other associated substances. This is true of cholesterol, which is linked to health problems such as coronary heart disease and high blood pressure. It is found mainly in fat products from animal sources such as fatty meat, butter and eggs.

Fat has the following functions in the body:

- it provides a concentrated source of energy
- it provides vitamins A and D
- it is stored in the tissues and keeps us warm.

Young children need a certain amount of fat to function, but if the intake is too high they will store the surplus as body fat and put on weight. Fried foods should be avoided for this reason.

KEY POINTS

- **Foods contain a range of nutrients.**
- **The body needs macronutrients in large amounts.**
- **Protein is needed for the growth and repair of body tissues.**
- **Fats and carbohydrates provide the body with energy.**
- **Dietary fibre (NSP) helps the digestive system work properly.**

KEY TASKS

1 **Explain the term 'protein complementation'.**
2 **Why are unprocessed sources of carbohydrate, such as wholewheat flour, better for young children?**
3 **Explain why young children need a high protein intake.**
4 **Plan the meals for a day for a child aged 3–4 years. Explain where each nutrient is provided.**

Nutrition (2)

MICRONUTRIENTS

Micronutrients are the vitamins and minerals that are needed in much smaller quantities but which are still important for the body. Vitamins and minerals carry out a number of essential functions and often work with other nutrients.

Deficiency diseases

Deficiency diseases are caused by a shortage of a nutrient. Anaemia is a deficiency disease caused by a lack of iron in the diet. A low intake of calcium means that less calcium is deposited in the bones, which leads to weakness in the skeleton. Severe calcium shortage could result in rickets.

DIETARY REFERENCE VALUES

The amount of nutrients needed by babies and young children in their diet is calculated using **dietary reference values (DRVs)**. DRVs are measures of the amounts of a nutrient or energy needed by a person to be healthy.

DRVs are calculated as daily average amounts for population groups (a group of people with similar nutritional and energy needs, such as two-year-old children). It is important to know how nutritional values are calculated using DRVs to help understand the value of foods in the diet.

There is a range of different DRV measures such as reference nutrient intake (RNI) and estimated average requirement (EAR).

Reference nutrient intake (RNI) is the amount of a nutrient, e.g. protein, that is needed by a population group. For example, the RNI for a six-month-old baby is 12.7 grams of protein per day (see table below). This means that a baby of this age needs

RNI of protein for children under six years of age

Age of child	Grams/day
4–6 months	12.7
7–9 months	13.7
10–12 months	14.9
1–3 years	15.5
4–6 years	19.7

that amount of protein for the growth and repair of their body.

Estimated average requirement (EAR) is an estimate of the average requirements for a population group such as a 12-month-old baby. As it is the average, it means that some babies will need more than the EAR and some will need less. The following table shows the amount of kilocalories/kilojoules needed to provide for the energy needs of babies and young children.

EAR of kilocalories/kilojoules for children under six years of age

Age of child	Boys		Girls	
	kJ/day	kcal/day	kJ/day	kcal/day
0–3 months	2280	545	2160	515
4–6 months	2890	690	2690	645
7–9 months	3340	825	3200	765
10–12 months	3850	920	3610	865
1–3 years	5150	1230	4860	1165
4–6 years	7160	1715	6460	1545

THE ENERGY VALUE OF FOODS

All macronutrients, protein, fats and carbohydrates provide the body with energy. Fats provide twice as much energy as carbohydrates and proteins, so fat is the most concentrated source of energy.

Nutrients are broken down and used by the body to provide energy for:

- activities
- maintaining body temperature
- other body processes such as growth and repair, breathing and circulation.

Children vary in the amount of energy they need. Energy requirements vary because:

- some children are more active than others
- boys have a higher basal metabolic rate than girls. This means that they use up energy at a faster rate than girls
- age and size or height will affect the amount of energy needed by the body.

Measuring energy in food

The energy in food is measured in kilocalories (kcal) or kilojoules (kJ).

1 kilocalorie = 4.2 kilojoules

Kilocalories can be converted to kilojoules by multiplying by 4.2. Food labels on baby and toddler food products usually give the energy value of the product in both kilocalories and kilojoules.

Energy balance

If young children eat more kilocalories than they use up in energy, they will put on additional weight. There are many overweight (obese) young children today because they have a diet that is high in energy-dense foods such as chips and sweets, and high-fat, fast foods such as burgers. To maintain an energy balance during childhood, it is necessary to balance the kilocalories taken in as food with the kilocalories used as energy for activities. When there is an energy imbalance, the body will become overweight or underweight.

As the eating habits of many families have changed over recent years, with a greater emphasis on snacking, convenience foods and eating out, it has become more difficult for children to achieve a healthy balance.

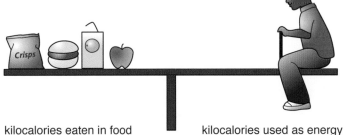

kilocalories eaten in food   kilocalories used as energy

Energy balance

Lack of activity

In the past many children would lead an active lifestyle, which included lots of physical activity and exercise. Today some children spend more time watching television or playing on computer games than running about or doing exercise. As a result, fewer calories are used, leading to weight gain and obesity (when a person's weight is a third more than average for their age and size).

Fewer children and families walk or ride bikes, as they rely more on the family car for transport. It is very important that parents should consider how much physical activity their child undertakes. Every exercise opportunity should be taken to try to develop the child's fitness and to give them an active lifestyle, so that they do not get used to sitting for hours at a time. For example, a bike ride, a regular

walk to school, playing in the park, taking part in football or other team games all encourage the child to have a more active approach to life.

FOR FURTHER REFERENCE All of the latest recommendations can be found on the Food Standards website (see our hotlinks website).

KEY POINTS

- Vitamins and minerals are micronutrients needed in small amounts by the body.
- Deficiency diseases are caused by a shortage of a nutrient.
- Dietary reference values (DRVs) are measures of the amount of a nutrient or energy needed.
- To maintain an energy balance, the kilocalories taken in as food need to be balanced with the kilocalories used as energy for activities.
- Many children today would benefit from a more active lifestyle.

KEY TASKS

1 What are dietary reference values?
2 Why is it important to maintain an energy balance?
3 Explain why the energy requirements of babies and young children will vary.
4 Describe how modern lifestyles contribute to the problems of weight gain in children.

GradeStudio

Try this practice question:

Poor eating habits have led to an increase in obesity in children.

1 Explain what is meant by the term 'obesity'. (2 marks)
2 Describe how obesity affects young children. (5 marks)
3 Explain how obesity can be avoided. (5 marks)

Think about it

How many obese young children do you know? Are their parents overweight also? Do you think that there are more obese children living in your area than there were a few years ago?

Nutrition (3)

We should eat a variety of foods every day to provide us with all of the different nutrients we need. If a nutrient is in short supply for any length of time, we will develop a deficiency.

'FIVE A DAY'

According to research, the average person in the UK eats fewer than three portions of fruit and vegetables a day, instead of the recommended five. Worryingly this is even lower among young people. It is important to encourage young children to try as many different fruits and vegetables as possible to encourage good eating habits for the future. That means five portions altogether, not five portions of fruit and five portions of vegetables.

> **Fruit and vegetables:**
>
> - are packed with vitamins and minerals
> - can help to maintain a healthy weight
> - are an excellent source of fibre and antioxidants
> - help to reduce the risk of heart disease, stroke and some cancers
> - taste delicious and there are loads to choose from.

The School Fruit and Vegetable Scheme is part of the five-a-day programme to increase fruit and vegetable consumption in children in the UK. Under the scheme, all children aged four to six years are entitled to a free piece of fruit or vegetable during each school day.

Eating a wide variety of fruit and vegetables provides children with plenty of vitamins and minerals, as many such foods are naturally high in folic acid, vitamin C and potassium. They are also a good source of fibre and antioxidants. These nutrients are all-important for children's health – not only now but for the future too.

Fruit and vegetables are generally low-fat, low-calorie foods (provided that they are not fried or roasted in lots of oil). Therefore, if children eat more fruit and vegetables instead of less healthy foods that are high in fat and added sugars, they can help to develop a healthier lifestyle and a good weight in the future.

🔑 KEY TASKS

Plan the meals for a family with three children for one day, including drinks and snacks, to ensure that they are all having 'five a day'.

Talk about it

How can you encourage children who say that they do not like fruit and vegetables to try something new?

Functions and sources of different nutrients

Nutrient	Function	Sources	Result of deficiency
Protein	Growth and repair of cells and body tissues	Animal: meat, milk, fish, cheese, eggs Plant: beans, peas, nuts, lentils, soya, quorn, textured vegetable protein (TVP), rice, cereals	Kwashiorkor (severe malnutrition showing pot-bellies swollen with water)
Fat	To provide energy and warmth	Animal: meat, oily fish, butter, cream, cheese, eggs, milk Plant: nuts, sunflower oil, olive oil, soya beans, rapeseed oil	
Fluoride	Helps to keep calcium in bones and teeth and helps to resist acid produced in the mouth by bacteria	Seafood, tap water, toothpaste	Tooth decay

Carbohydrates • Sugar	To provide energy. They also work with protein to aid growth and repair	Honey, fruit, chocolate, refined sugar, e.g. granulated	Failure to thrive, wasting of muscles, weight loss
• Starch		Flour, potatoes, pasta, rice, noodles, beans, cereals	
Vitamin A	Keeps skin, eyes and mucous membranes healthy	Butter, margarine, eggs, cheese, oily fish, carrots, green vegetables, apricots	Impaired vision, slow growth in children
Vitamin B group including folic acid	Helps the release of energy from food	Bread, wholegrain cereals, milk and milk products, meat, fish, eggs, pulses, yeast and yeast extracts	Beri-beri (degeneration of the nerves), pellagra (inflamed/flaky skin), diarrhoea, disorders of the nervous system, slow growth in children
Vitamin C	Helps in the absorption of calcium and iron. Helps wounds to heal and protects against infections and allergies	Citrus fruits, strawberries, tomatoes, green vegetables, potatoes, red and green peppers, blackcurrants	Poor skin, scurvy, slow-healing wounds
Vitamin D	Aids absorption of calcium	Margarine and low-fat spread, fatty meat, fish, eggs. Produced under the skin by the action of sunlight	Rickets
Iron	An important part of haemoglobin. Maintains cell functions	Red meat, cocoa, plain chocolate, watercress, white bread, green vegetables, hard water	Anaemia (reduction in the oxygen-carrying capacity of the blood)
Iodine	Needed for the development of the foetus's system, regulates metabolism and hormone production	Seafood, seaweed, milk	Goitre (abnormally enlarged thyroid gland)
Fibre/NSP (non-starch polysaccharide)	Aids digestion and prevents constipation	Cereals, fruit and vegetables including the skins	Constipation

Healthy eating

DIETARY GOALS

Dietary goals are targets that are set to improve the health of people in the UK.

DIET-RELATED ILLNESS

Many diseases today are related to our eating habits. They are called **diet-related illnesses** for this reason. Healthy eating habits that are established while children are young will reduce their chances of developing a diet-related illness such as coronary heart disease. Diets that are high in calories and fat and low in dietary fibre may result in health problems such as obesity, coronary heart disease and diabetes later in life.

One factor thought to trigger type 2 diabetes is being overweight. Diabetes is when the body has a high level of glucose in the blood. Type 2 diabetes is a form of diabetes that develops later in life and is related to diet. This can lead to damage to the kidneys, nervous system and heart.

Heart disease

Heart disease covers a range of conditions varying from coronary heart disease and strokes to hypertension.

Coronary heart disease and strokes are linked to many factors, one of which is a high level of cholesterol in the blood. The liver uses the fat we eat to produce cholesterol. This is a fat-like substance that gets deposited on the walls of the arteries when the level of blood cholesterol is high. The arteries become narrower and restrict the flow of blood around the body. In some cases this can lead to a heart attack.

Hypertension is often referred to as high blood pressure and means that a person's blood pressure

> Other factors that can contribute to coronary heart disease and strokes include:
> - being overweight
> - high blood pressure
> - smoking
> - lack of activity and exercise.

is very high. The blood is forced through the arteries at a higher pressure than normal and this puts extra strain on the heart. Hypertension can be caused by high cholesterol and high levels of salt in the diet. It can lead to heart attacks. People with hypertension need to follow a low-fat and low-salt diet.

Low-fibre diets

It is estimated that over a third of the population of the UK has too low an intake of dietary fibre (NSP). Dietary fibre is needed to make sure the digestive system functions properly and to prevent bowel conditions such as constipation, diverticular disease and bowel cancer. Diets containing prepared food products are more likely to be low in fibre.

CHILDHOOD OBESITY

Children's diet affects their health in the long and short term. The number of children who are overweight is increasing – it is estimated that at least one child in five is overweight. The term 'obesity' refers to a person whose weight is at least a third more than the average weight for their age and size.

Many foods that appeal to young children are energy dense and nutrient scarce, such as high-

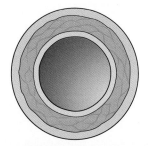

Healthy artery allows blood to flow

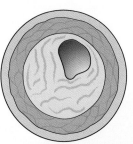

Artery narrowed by cholesterol deposits

Energy dense and nutrient scarce foods are not good for children

sugar drinks. This means that they are high in calories but low in other nutrients. Young children do need high levels of energy, but it is better to obtain this from foods that also contain other nutrients such as brown bread, pasta and other cereals. If a child eats food containing more calories than they use in energy, they will put on weight.

Overweight children become less active and this can lead to further weight gain. The extra weight can put a strain on the heart and blood circulation which can, in turn, lead to other health problems later in life. Many children are overweight because they have too high an intake of sugar and fat.

SUGAR IN THE DIET

Children like sweet tastes. Both breast and formula milk have a sweet taste because of the lactose present in it. Sugar is often called an empty calorie food because it provides the body with energy but not with any other nutrients. Most sweet products that children like have sugar added in the manufacturing process. These sugars are called extrinsic sugars (added sugars) and can be harmful to their teeth. Natural sugars present in foods such as fruit and vegetables are less harmful to the teeth. They are called intrinsic sugars.

How is sugar harmful to the teeth?

Diets that are high in sugar can cause plaque to form. Plaque is formed when bacteria in the mouth

convert the sugar to acid. This can attack the enamel of the teeth, causing dental cavities.

LINK For more information on caring for the teeth see page 59.

Parents and carers should follow these guidelines to help reduce the sugar levels in children's diets:

- give young children diluted, unsweetened fruit juices to reduce the sugar levels, rather than squashes and fizzy drinks, or let them drink water
- avoid adding extra sugar to hot drinks
- limit the amount of sweet foods such as confectionery, chocolate, biscuits and cakes
- substitute sugary foods with other low-sugar snacks, such as pieces of fresh fruit or vegetables, unsweetened yoghurts or savoury biscuits.

KEY POINTS

- **Diet-related illnesses are medical conditions that are related to the foods we eat.**
- **What children eat affects both their short-term and their long-term health and well-being.**
- **Many children are overweight because they eat too much sugar and fat.**

KEY TASKS

1 **Explain the term 'diet-related illness'.**
2 **Describe the causes of the following:**
   a **Coronary heart disease.**   c **Diverticular disease.**
   b **Hypertension.**
3 **Why is too much sugar unhealthy for young children's teeth?**
4 **Explain the differences between intrinsic and extrinsic sugars.**
5 **What is a 'sweet tooth'?**

Levels of sugar in foods

Food product	Teaspoonfuls of sugar per portion
Cocoa	3
Flavoured yoghurt	2
Cheese sandwich on white bread	4.5
Jelly and ice cream	4.5
Can of cola	7
Baked beans	2
Chocolate crispy cereal	3
Burger in a bun	1.5
Ketchup	1
Tinned fruit in syrup	6
Fresh orange juice	3

Talk about it

Why is it better for young children to have more starchy carbohydrate foods than sugary foods in their diet?

In your group spend a few minutes discussing this and preparing your most important point to report back to the class.

A balanced diet

Healthy eating habits in childhood should help to reduce the risk of diet-related illnesses in later life. Children should be given lots of fruit and vegetables to eat and should be encouraged to try a wide range of different foods. Activities such as cooking together, growing vegetables in the garden and shopping together all encourage children to develop healthy attitudes to food. Parents and carers need to understand the concepts of nutrition so they can plan a varied balanced diet for their children. A balanced diet contains the right amount and proportions of nutrients. Dietary reference values (DRVs) can be used to help make sure the diet of a child is nutritionally sound.

HEALTHY EATING GUIDELINES

There are many approaches to planning healthy diets for children. The eatwell plate is a guide to food selection that has been developed by the Food Standards Agency. The plate shows the types and proportions of foods we need for a healthy and well-balanced diet. For example, it shows that we should be eating a variety of types of food, including lots of fruits and vegetables, starchy foods and wholegrain cereals, some protein-rich foods and some dairy products.

The eatwell plate, Food Standards Agency

The eatwell campaign supports the government's guidelines for a healthy diet and offers eight tips:

- base your meals on starchy food
- eat lots of fruit and vegetables
- eat more fish

- cut down on saturated fat and sugar
- eat less salt – no more than 2 g per day for children 1–3, 3 g for children aged 4–6 and 5 g for those aged 7–10
- get active and try to be a healthy weight
- drink plenty of water
- do not skip breakfast.

These healthy eating guidelines are not intended to apply in full to young children under five. This is because young children have high energy requirements for their body weight. However, a sensible family eating pattern based on these guidelines will encourage children to eat healthily at home and establish good eating habits.

PLANNING MEALS

When planning family meals, there are some basic guidelines to consider:

- include proteins, calcium, iron, and vitamins A and D which are essential for growing children. The rapid growth of early childhood requires nutrient-dense foods that are rich in essential macro- and micronutrients
- include high-fibre food in their diet in a form that is appropriate for their age. Vegetables and fruits will be puréed during the early stages of weaning, but firmer textures should be gradually introduced for a toddler to learn to chew properly
- whole milk is recommended for children as a main drink. Semi-skimmed and skimmed milk do not provide enough energy or vitamin A. Semi-skimmed milk may be given to children over the age of two
- a variety of foods should be given to children at an early age to get them used to a range of tastes and textures, as **food preferences** (the foods a child likes or dislikes) are established in early childhood
- choose healthier methods of cooking such as grilling or baking rather than frying (which adds extra fat)
- young children need plenty of liquids to maintain their fluid balance. They should be encouraged to drink water and unsweetened drinks as well as milk, rather than fizzy and sugary drinks
- mealtimes should be at regular times with limited snack foods in between

- young children have small appetites. Serve small, attractive portions – they can always have more later
- make family meals happy, social occasions that the young child will look forward to and enjoy
- encourage children to be independent in feeding themselves as early as possible.

LEARNING TO FEED THEMSELVES

When young children start learning to feed themselves they will get very messy. Parents and carers can help young children to learn by providing small cutlery and a dish with straight sides for the child to push the food up against. With encouragement young children soon learn to feed themselves.

At 12 months babies will mainly use their hands to feed themselves. By two years children can use a spoon well and may manage a fork. They can lift up a cup with two hands. By the time they are three years old they can use a fork and spoon with precision. When they are four years old they can use a knife, fork and spoon and serve themselves from dishes. They may still need help cutting up difficult food.

PREPARED FOOD PRODUCTS

Modern family lifestyles have cut down on the time available for cooking meals. Many parents and carers have limited time to cook and prepare meals and rely on ready meals. Many prepared food products are high in fat and sugar. However, some can be used as part of a balanced diet, for example baked beans, fish fingers, tinned fish and wholegrain breakfast cereals.

When children learn to feed themselves they get messy

When using prepared food products, remember:

- read the labels carefully to understand what they contain
- use with fresh foods
- avoid any products that are high in fat, salt or sugar
- try to add additional textures to serve with the products
- grill, bake or microwave the products rather than frying.

FOR FURTHER REFERENCE
Find out more about the Nursery milk scheme and the Welfare food scheme.

More information about the milk initiative in schools can be found on the National Dairy Council website (see our hotlinks website).

KEY POINTS

- A balanced diet contains the right amount and proportions of essential nutrients.
- Parents and carers should do their best to make sure children eat a balanced diet.
- Some ready-made foods can be used as part of a balanced diet.

KEY TASKS

1 Explain why young children should drink whole milk.
2 What is the eatwell plate? Explain how it can be used to plan healthy, balanced meals for young children.
3 Prepare a checklist to identify the key points to consider when planning meals for young children.
4 a Plan a two-course meal for a 14-month-old child. What nutrients does your meal supply?
  b What other foods would the child need to be given during the course of the day to ensure it has a good balance?

FURTHER WORK

Create a design for a simple jigsaw or domino game for a four-year-old child to help them understand about healthy eating.

Diet-related issues

FOOD REFUSAL

Food refusal is the term used when a child refuses to eat their food. This happens most commonly between the ages of nine months and four years.

There are several reasons why a child may refuse food:

- children go through development stages where they will not co-operate with others – it is normal for children to say 'no' and refuse to do something
- children enjoy mealtimes as an experience and enjoy playing with the food as much as eating it
- children may not like the taste of the foods they have been given to eat
- some children have small appetites and do not want or need large quantities of food
- some young children may see food refusal as a way of seeking attention.

Parents and carers worry when a toddler refuses to eat. They feel anxious and under pressure to make sure their child eats a nutritionally adequate diet. But all children are individuals with their own likes and dislikes, and their tastes change – a food they do not like one week may be eaten the next. When children are hungry they will eat. Very few children become ill because of food refusal. Parents and carers who are concerned can ask for advice from their doctor, health clinic or health visitor.

There are many reasons why a young child may refuse food

> **Medical advice that is given to parents and carers about food refusal by child health specialists is:**
>
> - make mealtimes relaxed, social occasions where young children are encouraged but not forced to eat
> - do not give snacks between meals to children who do not eat at mealtimes
> - if a child fails to gain weight as they grow, contact a doctor or health visitor.

FOOD INTOLERANCE

Food intolerance is a reaction to a food or an ingredient in the food product. Food allergy is a type of food intolerance caused by a reaction in the body to a specific food. Food intolerance can produce a wide range of symptoms in babies and young children such as skin rashes, abdominal cramps and more serious reactions. Foods that cause intolerance in babies and young children include milk, wheat, nuts, eggs and fish.

Foods that can cause intolerance or allergies in babies and young children

Type of intolerance	Foods to avoid
Cows' milk	Cows' milk and milk products such as cream, cheese and butter
Eggs	Eggs and the food products made from eggs such as cakes
Tartrazine	Foods containing tartrazine (E102) or other dyes (food colourings)
Gluten	Cereal products containing gluten, such as bread, and other baked products made from wheat, oats, barley or rye
Peanut	Peanuts and food products containing peanut products such as mayonnaise (which contains peanut oil)

It is known that babies who are weaned early are more likely to develop a food intolerance or be allergic to a particular ingredient or food product. It is thought that this is because the baby's body has not yet developed the ability to digest the particular food.

Young children often grow out of their allergies by the time they start school. Cows' milk intolerance is a common disorder in babies, as it has a different composition to breast milk.

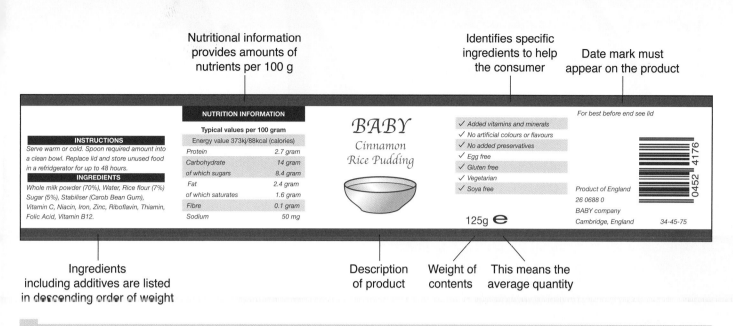

Nutritional information provides amounts of nutrients per 100 g

Identifies specific ingredients to help the consumer

Date mark must appear on the product

NUTRITION INFORMATION	
Typical values per 100 gram	
Energy value 373kj/88kcal (calories)	
Protein	2.7 gram
Carbohydrate	14 gram
of which sugars	8.4 gram
Fat	2.4 gram
of which saturates	1.6 gram
Fibre	0.1 gram
Sodium	50 mg

INSTRUCTIONS
Serve warm or cold. Spoon required amount into a clean bowl. Replace lid and store unused food in a refridgerator for up to 48 hours.

INGREDIENTS
Whole milk powder (70%), Water, Rice flour (7%) Sugar (5%), Stabiliser (Carob Bean Gum), Vitamin C, Niacin, Iron, Zinc, Riboflavin, Thiamin, Folic Acid, Vitamin B12.

BABY
Cinnamon
Rice Pudding

125g ℮

✓ Added vitamins and minerals
✓ No artificial colours or flavours
✓ No added preservatives
✓ Egg free
✓ Gluten free
✓ Vegetarian
✓ Soya free

For best before end see lid

0452 4176

Product of England
26 0688 0
BABY company
Cambridge, England   34-45-75

Ingredients including additives are listed in descending order of weight

Description of product

Weight of contents

This means the average quantity

Labels provide valuable information to parents and carers when purchasing food products for children

Coping with a food intolerance

Parents and carers can get specialist help and advice about coping with a food allergy or intolerance from the community dietician. A wide variety of products are available in the supermarket and specialist stores to meet the needs of babies and young children with food allergies and intolerance.

FOOD LABELS

Food product labelling has improved in recent years, along with understanding of food intolerances. Parents and carers can use the nutritional information on the food label to:

- identify any particular ingredient that might cause an allergy or intolerance (all ingredients are stated on the product)
- consider the proportion of nutrient in the product as a percentage of the daily requirement
- check which ingredients are present in order of weight.

Specialist products are available for children with food intolerance

KEY POINTS

- Food intolerance is a reaction to a food or an ingredient in a food product.
- Foods that commonly cause food intolerance include milk, eggs, nuts and wheat. Specialist products are available for children who have a food intolerance.
- Labels give essential information to parents and carers about the content of food products.

KEY TASKS

1 a What is food refusal?

   b Suggest some reasons why children refuse food.

2 What advice is given to parents and carers by child health specialists about dealing with food refusal?

3 Explain what information can be found on a food product label.

4 Think of two examples of a food intolerance. For each, state the cause of the intolerance and then suggest ways that parents/carers can make adaptations to deal with the situation.

Think about it

Would you be able to deal with a food intolerance reaction?

- What happens?
- What should you do?
- Where can you get help?
- How can it be prevented?

Food preparation

Food for babies and young children must be prepared in a clean and safe environment as they are very vulnerable to infection. Food hygiene is therefore extremely important and a priority in the baby's first year of life.

FOOD POISONING

Food products are a source of nutrients for bacteria. If food becomes contaminated with bacteria and is given the correct conditions for growth, the bacteria will multiply rapidly. As bacteria multiply they produce toxins, which are poisons. This is called **food poisoning** and it is the most common illness in the UK.

Babies and young children have little resistance to these bacteria and many become seriously ill with gastroenteritis or other similar food-borne diseases.

Gastroenteritis

Every year a number of babies develop this illness. It is more common in bottle-fed babies than in those who are breastfed. This is because there is a greater chance of formula milk being infected during its preparation. Gastroenteritis is an inflammation of the stomach and it is caused by toxins (poisons produced by bacteria). The symptoms of the illness are vomiting and diarrhoea. The baby will become dehydrated very quickly. This is a serious condition and requires immediate medical help.

HOW FOOD BECOMES INFECTED

Food purchased in a shop should be safe to eat. Food manufacturers and retailers have to follow strict legal guidelines about the preparation, processing and storage of food – for example, ready-made formula feed is sterile until opened. It is usually after the purchase of the food product that contamination by bacteria occurs.

Bacteria will thrive where they have:

- warmth – temperatures above 5°C (although very high temperatures destroy bacteria)
- foods that they use as a source of nutrients such as milk, meat and eggs
- moisture which they need to grow – which is present in most foods.

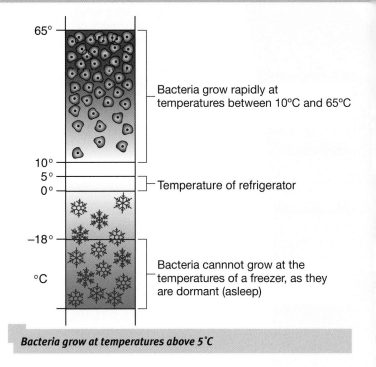

Bacteria grow rapidly at temperatures between 10°C and 65°C

Temperature of refrigerator

Bacteria cannnot grow at the temperatures of a freezer, as they are dormant (asleep)

Bacteria grow at temperatures above 5°C

FOOD HYGIENE FOR YOUNG BABIES

Young babies are vulnerable to food poisoning. Extra care must be taken when preparing bottle foods as milk is an ideal food for bacteria. Babies and young children always want to put objects in their mouths and they will gradually build up resistance to many bacteria. It is important that any surfaces and objects that they use are kept clean to reduce the risks where possible.

Food safety points to remember include the following:

- keep food cold to prevent the growth of bacteria – the fridge should be at a constant temperature of between 0 and 5°C
- keep food covered to prevent cross-contamination
- food handlers should always keep their hands clean by washing them in between preparing food.

CROSS-CONTAMINATION

Much of our food naturally contains some bacteria which are not harmful – for example, yoghurt or cheese. Many raw foods, particularly meats, contain bacteria which are destroyed during the cooking process. Foods which are most likely to be contaminated should be stored in a fridge. Other food should be kept clean by covering it to prevent **cross-contamination**. This is the transfer of bacteria from raw contaminated food to other foods.

Cross-contamination case study

This case study is an example of cross-contamination where bacteria from one food (the raw chicken) transfers to another (the egg sandwich).

Raw chicken contaminated with salmonella bacteria is prepared on a chopping board before being put in a casserole to cook. Then the same knife is used to cut and prepare egg sandwiches for a young child's tea. The sandwich is left on a plate in the kitchen for half an hour before tea. The bacteria contaminate the sandwich and grow rapidly in the warm kitchen environment. The child develops the symptoms of food poisoning later that day.

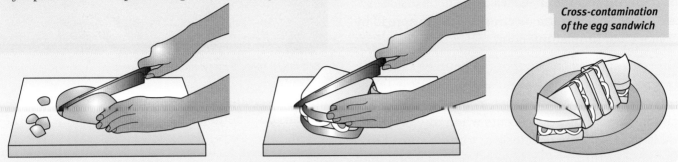

Cross-contamination of the egg sandwich

Other ways that cross-contamination can occur include the following:

- hands that are not washed between handling raw and cooked foods
- liquid from raw meat that drips on other foods in the fridge
- knives that are used with raw and cooked food without being washed
- dishcloths used to wipe down food surfaces can spread contamination.

BACTERIAL INFECTION IN THE HOME

Family pets should not be allowed in food preparation areas, as they can carry and transfer bacteria to surfaces. Flies can contaminate food by transferring bacteria from one source to another, for example from a dustbin outside to a child's feeder mug. People with coughs and colds can transfer infection to food by coughing or sneezing over it.

LINK For more information on infections see pages 98–99.

KEY POINTS

- Careful food storage reduces the risk of food poisoning.
- Cross-contamination of food is the transfer of bacteria from raw contaminated foods to other foods.
- Babies and young children are vulnerable to food poisoning.

KEY TASKS

1 List and explain the different ways that cross-contamination of food can occur.
2 Explain why food hygiene is important for babies.
3 What conditions do food poisoning bacteria need to grow?
4 How can gastroenteritis be avoided?

FURTHER WORK

Design a simple poster for the local clinic to explain the dangers of poor food hygiene when preparing food.

Think about it

Where and how is food poisoning most likely to occur in the home?

Response to infection

HOW DISEASE SPREADS

As children grow they are likely to suffer from one or more **infectious diseases**. Infectious diseases are caused by bacteria or viruses and are spread by contact and droplet infection.

Diseases such as chickenpox (sometimes called contagious diseases) are spread by contact with the infected child or articles such as toys used by the child. Droplet infection occurs when tiny drops of moisture containing bacteria or viruses spread from the nose or throat of an infected person when they cough or sneeze.

Incubation period

When the child is infected the bacteria or virus will multiply and grow. The incubation period is the time between catching the illness and the appearance of the first symptoms of the disease. Symptoms are the changes in the child's body which show the disease, such as spots.

Infectious stage

At this stage the bacteria can spread from the child with the infection to others. The infectious stage usually happens towards the end of the incubation period and for up to a week after the symptoms first appear. Children are infectious before they develop the symptoms of the disease themselves. By the time the symptoms are evident, they may have infected other children. This is why childhood diseases spread rapidly.

PARENTAL RESPONSIBILITY

A reference book can help parents and carers identify the symptoms of an infectious disease.

If a child develops an infectious disease, the parents or carers should inform:

- their GP, who will treat the illness
- the playgroup, nursery, childminder or school the child attends
- parents and carers of other children with whom the child has been in recent contact.

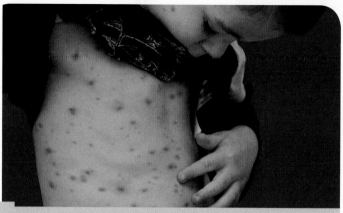

Red raised spots are a symptom of chickenpox

Most playgroups, nurseries and childminders have policies on whether they accept children when they are ill.

INFECTIOUS DISEASES

Meningitis

This is a very serious childhood infection caused by bacteria or a virus. It is the inflammation of the meninges, which is part of the brain and nervous system. Symptoms of the disease may include blotchy skin, fever and stiffness of the neck. A doctor will take immediate action if he or she suspects a child has the symptoms of meningitis, as it is an infection that develops very rapidly.

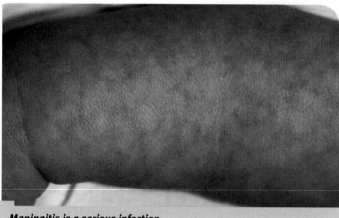

Meningitis is a serious infection

Coughs and colds

All children develop coughs and colds at some time. They are spread by droplet infection. Children are most likely to catch colds when they first start playgroup or school and mix with other children.

FOR FURTHER REFERENCE For more information on childhood ailments visit NHS Direct via our hotlinks website.

Common infectious childhood diseases

Disease	Incubation period	Symptoms	Treatment
Chickenpox	11–21 days	Child feels unwell. Slight rise in temperature. Rash appears in 24 hours with red raised spots that blister and form crusts	Treat spots with calamine lotion to stop itching. Give plenty to drink and paracetamol to lower temperature. Keep child in bed and away from pregnant women
Mumps	14–21 days	Slight fever and sore throat, with swelling on one or both sides of the jaw up to the ear. The child may have difficulty in chewing and swallowing	Give plenty to drink (but not fruit juices) and paracetamol to reduce pain. Keep child in bed
Rubella (German measles)	14–21 days	Slight rise in temperature followed by a rash of flat, pink spots on the face and body. Swollen glands in the neck are often present	Give plenty to drink. Keep child away from pregnant women
Whooping cough (pertussis)	7–14 days	Begins like a cold and cough, which gradually gets worse. Sometimes develops into a whooping noise. Coughing bouts make it difficult to breathe and may cause the child to choke and vomit	Antibiotics are often prescribed. The child needs plenty of rest and fluids. It will take a few weeks to recover
Measles	7–12 days	Begins like a bad cold and cough. Child becomes more unwell, with a temperature and sore, watery eyes. Rash appears with dark, blotchy (but not itchy) red spots on the face and neck, and then on the rest of the body	Measles can be a serious illness and the child needs careful nursing until their temperature drops. The room should be kept quiet and dark. Give plenty to drink and paracetamol to lower temperature

COMMON CHILDHOOD AILMENTS

Babies can develop other ailments, which are not infectious including:

- Colic. The baby will be uncomfortable and in pain because of a build-up of wind in the stomach. Winding a baby during feeding can help avoid colic. Simple remedies such as gripe water are available for colic. If the symptoms are severe, a doctor may prescribe drugs.

- Cradle cap. The baby develops a layer of scurf on the scalp. This is harmless and can be removed by softening with baby oil.

- Vomiting. Most babies vomit a small amount during and after feeding. More severe 'projectile' vomiting can be a symptom of a serious illness and a doctor should be consulted. Projectile vomiting causes the baby to dehydrate. It can be a symptom of food poisoning or gastroenteritis.

Other childhood ailments include:

- Asthma. There is an increase in the number of children suffering from asthma today. Asthma can be triggered by an allergic reaction or by an infection. Doctors prescribe treatment for asthma.

- Earache. Many children develop earache as a side effect of a cold or cough. This may develop into an inflammation of the inner ear and can be very painful for the child. Severe earache needs treatment from a doctor.

KEY POINTS

- Infectious diseases are spread by contact and droplet infection.
- The incubation period is the time between the first contact with the bacteria and the first symptoms of the disease.
- If a child develops an infectious disease the parents and carers should contact their GP.

KEY TASKS

1 How are infectious diseases spread?
2 Describe the symptoms of chickenpox and explain the treatment that parents and carers can give to the child.
3 Explain why it is important for parents and carers to inform the playgroup or school if their child has an infectious disease.
4 Design an informative method to inform parents about the symptoms of infectious diseases.

Immunisation

Immunity is the body's ability to resist infection. Immunity can be given to a child by immunisation. Children are given a vaccine that makes their bodies produce antibodies to fight infection. Immunisation is sometimes also called **vaccination**.

It is important to have babies immunised at an early age

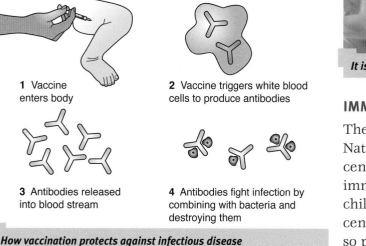

1 Vaccine enters body

2 Vaccine triggers white blood cells to produce antibodies

3 Antibodies released into blood stream

4 Antibodies fight infection by combining with bacteria and destroying them

How vaccination protects against infectious disease

Having children immunised gives extra protection against some very serious illnesses. The local child health clinic or GP arranges for immunisations to take place. This has resulted in many diseases like polio and diphtheria being rare in the UK. If babies and children are immunised at an early age, they are protected against the disease by the time they start playgroup and come into contact with lots of other children.

IMMUNISATION PROGRAMME

The immunisation programme is part of the National Health Service (NHS) provision. Health centres provide parents and carers with an immunisation record card to note down when their child is immunised. The record is also kept on a central database at the health centre or GP's surgery, so parents and carers can be advised when to bring in the child for the vaccine.

ROUTINE IMMUNISATIONS

The DTaP/IPV/Hib vaccine is offered to babies when they are two, three and four months old. This vaccine protects against diphtheria (D), tetanus (T), pertussis (whooping cough) (P), polio (IPV) and Hib (haemophilus influenzae type b). Diphtheria is a serious disease that can damage the heart and

Immunisation programme

When it is given	Diseases protected against	Vaccine given
2 months	• Diphtheria, tetanus, pertussis (whooping cough), polio and Hib • Pneumococcal infection	• DTaP/IPV/Hib • PCV
3 months	• Diphtheria, tetanus, pertussis (whooping cough), polio and Hib • Meningitis C	• DTaP/IPV/Hib • MenC
4 months	• Diphtheria, tetanus, pertussis (whooping cough), polio and Hib • Meningitis C • Pneumococcal infection	• DTaP/IPV/Hib • MenC • PCV
Around 12 months	• Hib and meningitis C	• Hib/MenC
Around 13 months	• Measles, mumps and rubella • Pneumococcal infection	• MMR • PCV
3 years and 4 months or soon after	• Diphtheria, tetanus, pertussis (whooping cough) and polio • Measles, mumps and rubella	• DTaP/IPV • MMR
Girls aged 12–13 years	• Cervical cancer caused by human papillomavirus types 16 and 18	• HPV
13–18 years	• Diphtheria, tetanus and polio	• Td/IPV

nervous system. Tetanus bacteria are found in soil and can enter the body through a cut. It is a painful disease that affects the muscles and can cause paralysis. Whooping cough can cause long bouts of coughing and choking that can make it hard to breathe. It can be serious in young babies. Polio is a virus that attacks the nervous system and can cause permanent muscle paralysis. DTaP/IPV is a pre-school booster vaccine given to children aged from three years and four months to when they start school.

The PCV vaccine protects against pneumococcal infection, which can cause diseases such as pneumonia, septicaemia and meningitis. Babies are offered PCV at two, four and around 13 months.

MenC is a vaccine offered to babies when they are three and four months old, with a dose of the combined Hib/MenC vaccine given at 12 months. This protects against infection by meningococcal group C, which can cause meningitis and septicaemia. The MenC vaccine does not protect against meningitis caused by other bacteria or viruses.

The first MMR vaccination is given to children at around 13 months of age and a second dose is given with the pre-school booster immunisation at three years and four months of age. It protects against measles, mumps and rubella (German measles). Measles is a serious disease that can lead to pneumonia and encephalitis, and it can kill. However, the debate about the possible side effects of the MMR vaccination has led to a decade of relatively low vaccination uptake, so the number of cases of measles is rising. In August 2008 the government launched a 'catch-up' campaign aimed at children up to the age of 18 who had not been not been fully vaccinated with MMR.

The HPV vaccine protects against the two strains of human papillomavirus that cause cervical cancer in over 70 per cent of women. It does not protect against any other sexually transmitted infections. It is offered to every girl in Year 12.

Td/IPV is a booster vaccine given to young people between the ages of 13 and 18. The vaccine tops up protection against tetanus, diphtheria and polio.

CONTRAINDICATIONS

Some parents and carers worry about their child's reaction to a vaccine. If they have reacted badly to a previous vaccine this is called a contraindication. Parents and carers can discuss with this their GP.

For a very small number of children there is a risk from side effects from the vaccine.

SHOULD CHILDREN BE IMMUNISED?

Some parents and carers wonder if they should immunise their children against diseases that are no longer common, such as polio and diphtheria. However, these diseases have been overcome because of the immunisation programme – if children are not immunised these diseases will become common again. There is much more risk to a child's health from the actual diseases than from the vaccines.

There are very few reasons why a child should not be immunised. Parents and carers should let the doctor or health visitor know if their child has a high fever, has had convulsions or fits or has reacted badly to previous vaccines.

KEY POINTS

- Immunisation protects the body against infections.
- The National Health Service provides an immunisation programme for children.
- Immunisation has made sure that diseases which were once common, such as diphtheria and polio, are now rare.
- A contraindication is a reaction to a previous vaccine.

KEY TASKS

1 Explain how a vaccine can prevent infectious diseases.
2 Why is it important that children are immunised before they start playgroup or nursery?
3 Why might some parents and carers not want their child to be immunised?
4 Describe the consequences of parents deciding against immunising their children.

FURTHER WORK

Visit your local health centre or primary care practice and see what information is available about immunisation programmes for children.

Think about it

- Should vaccinations be compulsory or should we have a choice?
- Are you aware of the MMR debate?

Caring for sick children (1)

All children get ill at some time in their childhood. When a normally lively child looks listless and unwell parents and carers can feel anxious. However most childhood illnesses pass quickly and help the child build up immunity to disease.

HOW TO TELL IF A CHILD IS UNWELL

When babies and young children are unwell they need special care. Usually it is easy to tell if a child is ill by their behaviour, which changes when they are becoming ill. Signs that a child is ill include:

- loss of appetite
- raised temperature
- flushed appearance
- tiredness
- being irritable
- crying.

Young babies cannot explain that they feel ill and they can develop infections rapidly.

> The following symptoms in a baby or child should prompt a parent or carer to get help immediately:
> - a fit, or if the child turns blue or very pale
> - a very high temperature (over 39°C), especially with a rash
> - difficulty in breathing
> - unusually sleepy or hard to wake up
> - a purple-red rash anywhere on the body, as this could be a sign of meningitis.

TAKING THE TEMPERATURE

Body temperature is a reliable sign that the child may be unwell. A child's temperature can vary anywhere between 36°C and 36.8°C. Parents and carers will need to take a young child's temperature as one way of finding out if the child is ill. There are several different types of thermometer available.

Taking a child's temperature

A digital thermometer offers the quickest, most accurate way to take a child's temperature and can be used in the mouth as follows.

1 Turn on the thermometer and clear it of any old readings.

Types of thermometer

Clinical A thin tube of glass with a bulb, usually containing mercury, at one end. When warmed the mercury expands and rises in the tube to display the temperature reading. Not recommended for use with young children.

Digital Digital thermometers are more expensive but easier to use. The heat of the body is read through a sensor and given as a digital reading.

Ear This type of digital thermometer is used by pointing it into the child's ear. It gives an accurate reading in seconds.

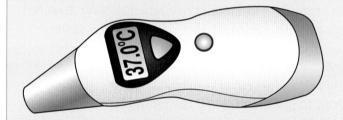

Strip The heat-sensitive strip is placed against the child's forehead and the body heat changes the colour of the strip to give a reading.

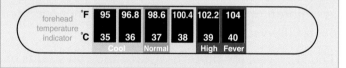

forehead temperature indicator	°F	95	96.8	98.6	100.4	102.2	104
	°C	35	36	37	38	39	40
		Cool		Normal		High	Fever

2 Put on a disposable plastic sleeve if the thermometer uses them or make sure the thermometer is clean.

3 Wait 20 minutes after the child has finished eating or drinking.

4 Place the tip of the thermometer under the tongue and ask the child to close the lips around it.

5 Wait until you hear the appropriate number of beeps to indicate that the temperature can be read.

A high temperature can be a sign that the child is unwell

If using a different type of thermometer follow the manufacturer's guidelines. Always clean thermometers before and after use.

A low temperature can be just as serious as a high temperature, as it can be an indication of hypothermia. Hypothermia is where the temperature of the whole body drops very low so the child gets extremely cold. Hypothermia is a serious condition and medical help must be given.

CHILDREN'S MEDICINE

It is usually best to consult a doctor before giving medicines to a baby or child. Most children's medicines are given in the form of syrup, often sugar free. If they are given in tablet form they must be crushed before they are given to the child.

Guidelines for giving medicines to a child include these safety points:

- read the instructions on the packet carefully
- make sure the instructions are followed closely about the timing and dosage of the medicine
- unless instructed otherwise, complete the course of the medication even if the child appears to have recovered
- store medicines in a safe place, out of reach and locked away from children, to avoid accidental poisoning
- throw away old medicines (or take them to the pharmacy) as out-of-date medicines are not effective.

WHEN TO CALL A DOCTOR

Parents and carers are usually the best judges of when the child is unwell. They will know when they need to contact the doctor. Most surgeries will allow the parent or carer to speak to the doctor on the phone if the doctor is not available immediately. If help is required outside surgery hours the NHS Direct helpline is available (0845 4647).

Parents and carers need to be able to give the doctor the following information:

- the child's symptoms
- how long the child has had these symptoms
- the child's temperature and whether it is continuing to rise
- the length of time the child has had the high temperature.

KEY POINTS

- **All children become ill at some point in their childhood.**
- **A high temperature is a reliable sign that a child is ill.**
- **Doctors should be consulted before giving medicine to children.**

KEY TASKS

1 **How can you tell if a baby or child is unwell?**
2 **What is the benefit of having a thermometer in the home to take the child's temperature?**
3 **Explain the guidelines for giving medicine to a child.**
4 **Research and describe how to take the temperature of a toddler, explaining which thermometer you would use and why.**

Think about it

How would you know the difference between a child feeling unwell and a child being *seriously* ill? Would you be able to recognise the signs or symptoms?

Caring for sick children (2)

A sick child needs:

- rest and sleep in a quiet room
- medication prescribed by the doctor
- plenty of fluids to drink
- a warm and draught-free room at about 22°C
- comfort and reassurance from the family.

When children are ill, they need a lot more attention and care. When they are awake they may want the company of others for reassurance. Left alone they may be fretful and demanding. Special toys and games can be used to try to occupy the child. How much activity they can cope with will depend on the stage of the illness.

Illness can often resort in the child being upset. Children get worried when they feel unwell and need comfort and cuddles to reassure them. If a child is well enough, they may enjoy company, such as visits from grandparents or friends. This will stop them feeling lonely and keep them entertained.

When children are unwell they will want activities they can watch rather than actively participate in, such as having stories read, watching television, listening to CDs and looking at books. When they are getting better they will enjoy participating more with jigsaws, crayoning books or construction toys, depending on the age of the child. The best place for a sick child is secure at home in his or her own bed or snuggled up on the sofa.

HOSPITAL

Sometimes babies and young children need to go to hospital. Up to 40 per cent of all children under the age of five have a hospital stay during their early childhood.

The main reasons why young children have to stay in hospital include:

- accidents that have caused injury such as broken bones or burns
- infections of the chest or stomach
- surgery for medical conditions
- medical care for congenital conditions.

A hospital stay is a difficult experience for a child. He or she is in different surroundings with a strange routine and different food. Most hospitals work together with the parents and carers to help the child settle in.

Support systems to enable parents and carers to stay with their children are usually available. Parents and carers should be able to be with their child whenever they like.

Recommendations are that:

- there is unlimited visiting for parents and carers of children in hospital
- provision is made for parents and carers to stay overnight with very young children whenever possible.

🔍 **FOR FURTHER REFERENCE** An organisation that supports the improvement of facilities for parents and carers is Action for Sick Children. Access its website via our hotlinks website.

A child feels secure at home in bed

Up to 40 per cent of children under five have a hospital stay

Preparing for a stay in hospital

It is important that the child is prepared for a hospital stay as it may be the first time he or she has been away from home and family. Hospitals can be frightening places for children as everything seems strange and unfamiliar.

> **It is a good idea to prepare children for the stay:**
>
> - talk about what will happen in hospital – the more you explain, the better the child will cope with the situation
> - explain about the jobs of nurses and doctors and other hospital staff
> - show the child books and tell them stories about being in hospital
> - encourage role-play games about hospitals
> - try to visit the hospital with the child beforehand and talk to staff about anything that will be important for your child such as particular likes and dislikes
> - let the child pack their own bag if possible to help them feel they are part of the process. Make sure they pack their favourite things such as special toys and books.

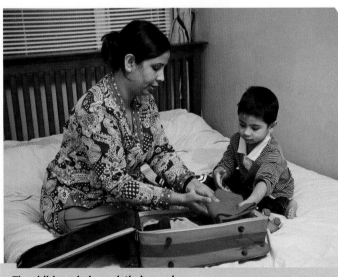
The child can help pack their own bag

Returning home from hospital

When the child returns home from hospital it will probably take them a while to settle back to the old routine. It is normal for children to become clingy or attention seeking afterwards. Reassurance and affection will help the child adjust back to their normal routine quite quickly.

REGRESSION

Any form of illness can affect a child's developmental progress. A severe or prolonged illness can actually cause the child to **regress**. Regression is when a child returns to behaviour they showed when they were younger. For example, a four-year-old who has had a prolonged hospital stay could start to have tantrums. When the child returns to normal health, he or she will soon start to make progress again.

> 🔑 **KEY POINTS**
>
> - A sick child will need more attention and care than normal.
> - The best place for a sick child is at home in bed where he or she feels secure.
> - Hospital stays are difficult for children, and parents and carers should be able to be with their child as much as is possible.
> - After a hospital stay children may find it difficult to adjust back to their routine.

> 🔑 **KEY TASKS**
>
> 1 Describe how to prepare a three-year-old child for a hospital stay.
> 2 Explain the needs of a sick child.
> 3 Why might a child regress after a prolonged stay in hospital?
> 4 💡 Outline how family members can help make the experience of going into hospital easier for a child to cope with.
> 5 💡 Design a table like the one below to identify the toys and activities that would be suitable to amuse a sick child, explaining your choices.
>
> | Age of child | Toy or activity | Reasons for choice |
> |---|---|---|
> | e.g. 12 months | | |

> **Talk about it**
>
> In pairs or groups suggest:
>
> - emergencies that could occur when a child may need urgent medical treatment
> - occasions when the child may go into hospital for a planned stay.

ExamCafé

Unit 4

Usha likes to revise with others; she hates working alone. It really suits her to devise a selection of questions and answers. She and her friends then question each other.

Everyone in the group thinks up three questions and answers then they question each other like this:

Q: Are deficiency diseases infectious or diet-related?
A: Diet-related.
Q: Why is calcium needed in the diet?
A: To build strong teeth and bones.
Q: What does a shortage of iron result in?
A: Anaemia.

> The thinking skills lesson we had was really good. We had to look at the foods that make up a balanced diet and then complete an eatwell plate. You have to look at the food and then decide where it goes. For example, cheese on toast goes in bread, rice, potatoes, pasta and other starchy foods and milk and dairy foods.
>
> You can draw out one of these and use it to revise lots of different topics.

 Kylie

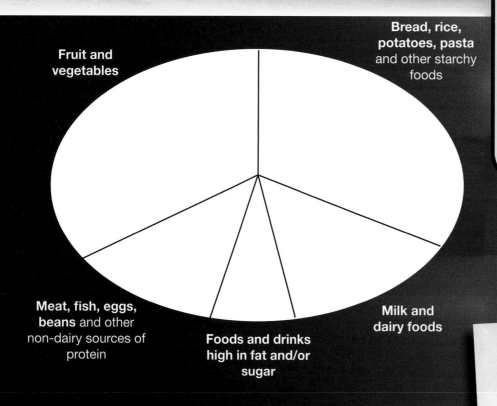

Fruit and vegetables

Bread, rice, potatoes, pasta and other starchy foods

Meat, fish, eggs, beans and other non-dairy sources of protein

Foods and drinks high in fat and/or sugar

Milk and dairy foods

Revision tip

Now for something completely different!

There are many different games that you can use to test your knowledge on up-to-date tips on healthy eating.

Log on to the government website accessed via our hotlinks website and see how many of them you can do!

Read through the foods listed below that combine to make up a balanced diet:

Rice pudding	Low-sugar fruit squash
Fish fingers	Strawberry and kiwi smoothie
Tuna sandwich	Mashed potato
Egg and soldiers	Pasta
Broccoli	Wholemeal toastie with cheese and onion
Cheese on toast	Ham sandwich
Vanilla milkshake	Yoghurt

Put them in the correct sections of the Venn diagram.

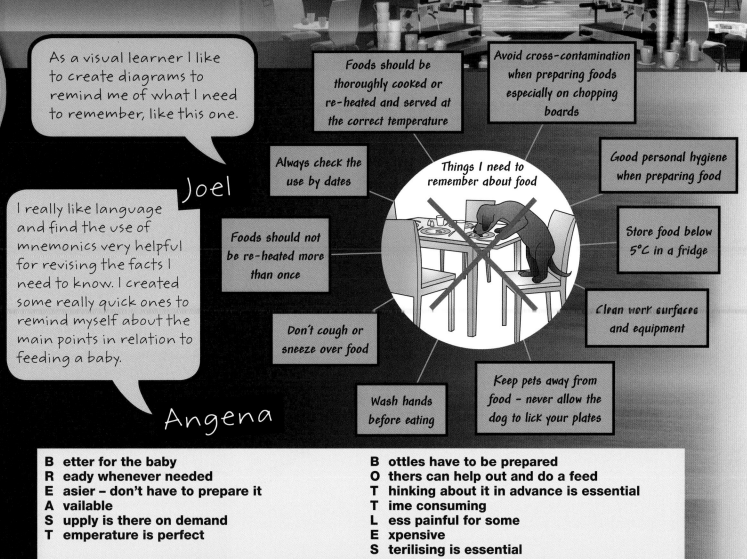

As a visual learner I like to create diagrams to remind me of what I need to remember, like this one.

Joel

Foods should be thoroughly cooked or re-heated and served at the correct temperature

Avoid cross-contamination when preparing foods especially on chopping boards

I really like language and find the use of mnemonics very helpful for revising the facts I need to know. I created some really quick ones to remind myself about the main points in relation to feeding a baby.

Angena

Always check the use by dates

Things I need to remember about food

Good personal hygiene when preparing food

Foods should not be re-heated more than once

Store food below 5°C in a fridge

Clean work surfaces and equipment

Don't cough or sneeze over food

Wash hands before eating

Keep pets away from food – never allow the dog to lick your plates

B etter for the baby	**B** ottles have to be prepared
R eady whenever needed	**O** thers can help out and do a feed
E asier – don't have to prepare it	**T** hinking about it in advance is essential
A vailable	**T** ime consuming
S upply is there on demand	**L** ess painful for some
T emperature is perfect	**E** xpensive
	S terilising is essential

You can use this technique for anything you like. Try it for yourself!

Revision checklist

Things I really need to remember…

Unit 4 revision checklist: feeding a baby		
Breastfeeding	• Provides colostrum • Provides antibodies • Best for the baby • Supply is always ready • Free • No sterilising of equipment • No preparation needed	☐☐☐☐☐☐☐
Bottle feeding	• Milk powder is modified to provide correct nutrients • Provides an opportunity for others to feed • More expensive • Equipment must be sterilised • Must be prepared according to instructions • Mum knows how much milk the baby has had	☐☐☐☐☐☐
Mixed feeding	• Should not start before the baby is four months old • When ready for weaning baby wants food more often • Baby shows signs of hunger after milk feed • Starts to wake up in the night hungry after sleeping through previously • Introduce new foods slowly – one at a time • Start with puréed fruit or vegetables • Use fresh foods whenever possible	☐☐☐☐☐☐☐

ExamCafé

Exam preparation

Here is an example of an essay-style question:

> Children who are ill usually feel miserable and may need more attention and care than usual.
>
> - Describe how to care for a child who feels poorly and is in bed at home. **(8 marks)**
>
> - Explain how a five-year-old child who is going into hospital can be prepared for their stay. **(8 marks)**

Student answer

When a child is ill, they generally need more love, attention and support than usual. When a child has to stay in bed they need to be in their own bed. They should be kept clean and comfortable so that they are not too hot and bothered and they don't get sweaty and sore. They need clean pyjamas and the bed sheets should be changed regularly. Even if the bed doesn't need to be changed it will need to be re-made and straightened, probably a couple of times a day, so that it isn't too rucked-up to lie on comfortably.

The room should be kept warm but it should also have the window open for some fresh air, so that the room is not too stuffy.

The child needs to wash its hands before eating and after using the toilet, especially if they are sick or have diarrhoea, to try to stop the spread of the infection. A bath will make them feel better and more comfortable but they don't need one every day unless they are very sweaty.

Children get really bored when they have to stay in bed so lots of interesting activities and books to read or colour are a good idea. It is nice if a grandparent or other visitor can visit to read to them. This will give the parent a break and give the child someone different to talk to. Children especially like to be spoiled by their grandparents and they can have little treats.

One thing that they should have lots of is drinks so that they don't get dehydrated. If the child has a high temperature or sickness this is really important as dehydration can be very serious and the child will recover more quickly if they are hydrated. They shouldn't be forced to eat if they don't feel like it and fluids should be given instead if they aren't eating. They need to have their temperature checked and if it is very high then they will need some paracetamol to try to get the temperature down. If they have a high temperature you could put them into a cool bath to try and cool them down. If a child's temperature gets really high then they can have fits.

If a child has to go into hospital you need to help them get used to the idea. You could read them a story about going to hospital or you could take them to have a look round so that they know what to expect when they go. They can take their teddy with them.

Look at these example exam questions and answers and think about the examiner's comments on the answers given.

a State the name given to milk powders designed for babies. **(1 mark)**
Formula/milk formula

Examiner says:
The only correct answer as brand names are not allowed.

b Equipment for bottle feeding must be sterile.
Name three methods of sterilising a feeding bottle. **(3 marks)**

1. Sterilising tablets/sterilising solution/chemical steriliser.
2. Steam sterilising.
*3. Boiling for at least 10 minutes (**not** just rinse with boiling water).*
4. Microwave steriliser.

Examiner says:
Any three from this list would make a good answer.

c Give three features you could expect to find in a well-designed
feeding bottle. **(3 marks)**
- *Wide neck.*
- *Well-fitting lid or cap so that it does not leak.*
- *Measurements on the bottle that are easy to read.*

Examiner says:
Other good answers would have been:
- Suitable shape/easy to hold
- **Clear** plastic to check it is clean (**not** just plastic)
- Correct size teats for the age of the baby
- A sealing disk to fit into the neck of the bottle so that it does not leak.

Key words	
amino acids	small component parts of a protein
colostrum	the first milk produced from the mother's breast after the birth of a baby
cross-contamination	the transfer of bacteria from raw, contaminated food to other foods
deficiency diseases	diseases caused by a shortage of a nutrient
dietary goals	targets set to try to improve people's health
dietary reference values (DRVs)	the amount of nutrients needed by population groups
diet-related illnesses	illnesses caused by the foods eaten in the diet
food intolerance	a reaction to a food or an ingredient in the food product
food poisoning	illness caused by eating contaminated food
food preferences	the foods a child likes or dislikes
food refusal	when a child refuses to eat its food
formula milk	milks and milk powders specially designed for babies
infectious diseases	diseases caused by bacteria or viruses, which can spread from person to person
macronutrients	nutrients that the body needs in large amounts, such as proteins, carbohydrates and fats
micronutrients	nutrients that the body needs in small quantities, such as vitamins and minerals
nutrition	the study of the nutrients found in the foods in our diet
regress	to go backwards in an area of development
vaccination	having an injection as a precaution against contracting a disease
weaning	when a baby's diet moves from just milk to solid food

Conditions for intellectual development

Intellectual development is the development of the mind. It is also known as **cognitive** development and is about the child's understanding, reasoning and learning.

> **Intellectual development depends on two main factors:**
> - the genes the child has inherited
> - the environment in which the child is brought up.

The terms '**nature**' and '**nurture**' are often used to describe these factors. Nature refers to the child's natural ability inherited from his or her parents and nurture refers to the way the child is stimulated and the amount of interaction that takes place with those around the child.

As with other areas of development, a child develops at his or her own pace, but the amount of stimulation and encouragement that a child receives will affect the learning process.

> **Conditions in which the child can develop to their full potential include an environment where:**
> - people talk and communicate
> - the child is offered visual stimulation, e.g. pictures, mobiles, toys to look at
> - the child is given love and security
> - the child is given a healthy diet.

Under these conditions the child is able to develop the following skills:

- concentration
- memory
- language
- creativity
- imagination
- the building up of **concepts** (ideas).

THE SENSES

The senses play an important part in a child's learning process. Children use all five senses – sight, smell, taste, touch and hearing – in order to develop.

Parents or carers can encourage and stimulate the child's senses by providing mobiles, a variety of toys and objects and by putting the child in positions where they can see what is going on around them.

Children learn by building one skill into another. For example, textures are important to young babies who enjoy the feel of different objects, whereas older babies will enjoy objects that can move around or make a noise. This is an example of a pattern of learning.

HOW CHILDREN LEARN

Children learn in a number of different ways.

Exploring

Children learn by exploring whatever is around them. When babies become mobile they should be offered toys and objects that are interesting, and the child will therefore gain information and knowledge. The greater the variety of objects, the more information the child will learn.

Babies learn by studying objects around them

Repetition

Children learn by listening to and looking at what is going on. If this is repeated time and time again (e.g. as in a nursery rhyme), they will learn and remember what is being said or what is happening. Memories are built up in this way. A memory will be used for storing and recalling information that can be used at a later date.

Imitation

Children develop intellectual skills by copying what they see and hear in their environment. A child learns new sounds, words and right from wrong by copying the people around them. Role-play – when children copy adult roles – is an important part of this learning process, e.g. dressing-up games, playing mummies and daddies, teachers or doctors and nurses.

Sharing a book is an enjoyable way for children to learn

PARENTS AND CARERS

Parents and carers have important roles to play in helping a child's intellectual development. They should provide stimulation, encouragement, support and opportunities to play as well as explaining information to the child and helping the child remember things.

PRE-SCHOOL

Pre-school groups are important for a child's early education. They build on the child's learning and offer a variety of stimulating activities in order for intellectual development to progress.

Looking at books

Children learn by sharing books with adults. Picture books, books that make sounds or which contain different textures are important for young babies. Older children will have books that include printed words, but pictures are still important. Reading stories to children helps them with listening skills, concentration and vocabulary.

Asking questions

When a child can talk, he or she will ask constant questions and these should be answered so that the child gains knowledge. Parents or carers must be patient and give answers that are clear.

Understanding concepts

Concepts are learned as children gain knowledge from playing and finding out about the world around them. Children begin to understand concepts such as heat, light and time as part of the learning process.

At around three years children will ask constant questions

![key icon] **KEY POINTS**

- A child's intellectual development is dependent on the genes inherited from the parents and the environment in which the child grows up.
- Children learn by exploring with their senses, through repetition, by imitation, by looking at books and by asking questions.
- Adults around the child can provide learning opportunities for the progression of intellectual development.

![key icon] **KEY TASKS**

1 What are the two main factors on which intellectual development depends?

2 How can a parent or carer provide the stimulation of a child's senses?

3 What part can a parent or carer play in helping a child's intellectual development?

4 List the different types of books that are available for young children.

Talk about it

'A bedtime story is valuable to both parent and child.' Discuss this statement.

FURTHER WORK

Find as many pictures as possible of different books. Sort them according to type, then arrange them on a sheet of paper, labelling them clearly.

Stages of intellectual development

As with all areas of development, there are intellectual development milestones which show the average age at which a child progresses. It must be remembered that the ages given below are only average ages, as all children are different and will develop their own rate.

Milestones of intellectual development include the following:

- newborn babies explore using their senses – sight, touch, hearing, smell and taste
- at one month, a baby will recognise their parent or carer
- at three months, a baby will play with their hands, take an interest in the surroundings and grasp objects
- by six months, a baby will want to be involved in an activity and will understand objects, e.g. if it is a musical toy the child will expect it to play music. The child will also show some understanding of the parent's or carer's voice, e.g. if the parent or carer is laughing
- at around nine months, babies can look in the direction of fallen toys, recognise familiar pictures, understand simple instructions and play 'not there' games, e.g. hide a toy and then look for it
- by 12 months, the baby can copy actions and treat objects in a relevant way, e.g. use a hairbrush correctly
- at 15 months, babies can remember people, recognise and sort shapes and understand the names of various parts of the body
- by 18 months, toddlers can recognise themselves in a photograph, begin to develop a memory for places and obey simple instructions
- at two years, the child can begin to understand the consequences of their actions, e.g. if they drop an object they know it may break and they can do simple jigsaw puzzles
- at two and a half years, the child will constantly ask questions, know their full name and notice details in pictures
- by around three years, the child will understand the concept of time, remember songs and nursery rhymes, recognise colours and compare sizes of objects
- by four years, the child can count up to 20, has developed memory skills, can solve simple problems, draw people and sort objects into groups
- at around five years, the child can produce detailed drawings, will act out adult roles with friends or alone, can understand past, present and future tenses and shows an interest in reading and writing.

MATHEMATICAL CONCEPTS

Sorting and counting are part of early mathematical development

Understanding numbers

The understanding of numbers is a gradual process for a child. Numbers regularly occur in conversation and in songs and stories, so the child will become aware of numbers in the everyday world around them. At around the age of two to three years, children can repeat numbers but do not understand what they mean. After this stage, children will learn how to match numbers with objects and then that numbers have an order.

Understanding size/mass and volume

This is also a gradual but important process in the development of a child's mathematical concepts. Providing the child is encouraged with a variety of activities, they will begin to recognise and compare size at an early age.

Bath toys and toys used in a sandpit, e.g. beakers and buckets, will encourage filling and emptying containers to help develop these concepts. Scales and stacking beakers will also help. Pre-school education offers facilities to help encourage these concepts in a child's intellectual development.

LEARNING TO DRAW

All children love to draw, and if they are encouraged and given materials, such as pencils, crayons and paper, they will draw and create pictures of the world around them. Drawing encourages fine manipulative skills as well as intellectual development. At around one year, if a child is shown how to hold a pencil, they will start to draw. A child can develop their imagination and express their feelings through drawing.

There are several stages of drawing, and many of these overlap, but there is a pattern in how children develop these skills. The first stages of drawing are a series of scribbles, and the control of the pencil or crayon is dependent on the child's manipulative skills.

The child produces scribbles by the hand moving backwards and forwards

The crayon can be lifted from the paper and it is moved in different directions

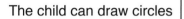

The child scribbles in circles

The child can draw circles

A circle is drawn with details of the eyes, nose and mouth

The child adds lines around the circle

The lines are arranged to represent the arms and legs

The child draws two circles to represent the head and the body. The arms are drawn coming out of the head

The legs have feet and the body is now important

Drawings are more detailed and include everyday items from the child's life, e.g. houses and trees

A child goes through a number of different stages when learning to draw

The development of language

The development of language and communication begins at birth. Babies are born with a need to communicate with other people before they can speak. They learn non-verbal messages from their parents and others around them. This is known as non-verbal communication.

A smiling baby is communicating with others

Babies communicate with others by:

- making noises
- using facial expressions
- making eye contact
- using their hands by pointing, touching and pulling at objects.

Babies start to learn to talk – verbal communication – very early. Children who are spoken to, or are in an environment where there is a lot of speech activity or stimulation, will develop language skills more quickly than those who are not stimulated with speech. As with all areas of development, children develop at their own pace.

Reasons why children develop at different rates include:

- boys tend to talk later than girls
- the baby may be concentrating on another aspect of development, e.g. walking
- an older brother or sister may 'talk' for the baby, so it may not need to talk
- there is a lack of stimulation from the family
- a hearing problem will cause the baby to miss the important stages in learning to speak.

STAGES OF LANGUAGE DEVELOPMENT (COMMUNICATION)

There are milestones, or norms, in the stages of communication development that all children pass through.

These are the average ages for the different milestones:

- newborn babies communicate by moving their legs and arms when responding to high-pitched tones, making eye contact and crying to show they are hungry
- at one month, the baby may make noises, e.g. gurgle, will respond to an adult by looking at them and will interact by cooing when spoken to
- at three months, the baby will smile, exchange noises with a familiar person and cry loudly
- at six months, the baby can make four sounds, e.g. 'goo', 'der', 'adah' and 'ka', looks for the source of sounds and will talk to themselves in a tuneful voice
- at around nine months, the baby may say words like 'dad-dad' and 'mum-mum' and will imitate sounds, e.g. a cough
- by 12 months, the baby will be able to follow simple instructions and can say 'bye bye'
- at around 15 months, the baby can join in with nursery rhymes and songs and respond to simple commands
- by 18 months, the toddler will babble sentences, say six or more words and respond to simple questions
- at around two years, the child can form two-word sentences, understand many more words than he or she can speak and will constantly name everyday objects

- by two and a half years, the child can use questions and pronouns, e.g. I, you, me, and say some rhymes and songs
- at around three years, the child can form three- to four-word sentences, tell stories, carry on simple conversations, have a vocabulary of up to 200 words and will learn more than one language if they live in a bilingual family
- by four years, the child can give descriptions of events that have taken place, match words with pictures, talk fluently, say his or her full name and address and enjoy jokes
- at five years, the child is fluent and grammatically correct in his or her speech, and shows an interest in language, reading and writing.

Children at 12 months can wave bye bye

HOW A CHILD LEARNS VERBAL COMMUNICATION

The baby learns to talk by making sounds and then learning to put them in order.

A baby with can be helped with verbal communication by:

- other people, especially adults, talking to the baby
- listening to sounds, e.g. music, voices and singing
- practising sounds itself
- copying sounds made by others.

If sounds are not made around the baby or child, it will not learn to speak very well. Babies and children need to be stimulated by parents or carers in order to develop their language. Interaction (talking with others, having conversations) with adults is an important part of a child's speech and vocabulary development.

Adults can help with speech and language development by:

- listening to the child
- being patient
- talking directly to the child
- repeating words and phrases
- praising and encouraging the child
- answering questions
- reading stories
- singing nursery rhymes.

KEY POINTS

- **Babies can communicate in a non-verbal way with other people.**
- **They learn language at an early age and, provided they are given stimulation with speech, they will develop through the milestones of communication with few problems.**
- **The rate of development may vary from child to child for a variety of reasons.**
- **Children who are not given any stimulation may have speech difficulties.**

KEY TASKS

1 **Give four ways a baby can communicate before they can speak.**
2 **Suggest three reasons why a child may be slow in their language development.**
3 **How can a child be helped to learn verbal communication?**
4 **Explain how adults can encourage a child's speech development.**
5 **Suggest some possible reasons that may prevent a child from learning to speak to others fluently.**

FURTHER WORK

Design and make a matching picture and word game that would encourage a child's speech development.

Unit 5: Intellectual, social and emotional development **115**

Speech problems and pre-reading skills

SPEECH PROBLEMS

Sometimes children may have problems in learning to speak. Children will only learn to speak if they can hear others speaking around them. They need to be stimulated by sounds and speech if progression in language development is to be made. It is natural for young children to make mistakes when they are learning to pronounce words and these **mispronunciations** usually disappear by the time the child is five years old.

> **Some common mispronunciations are:**
> - 'yeth' instead of 'yes'
> - 'lellow' instead of 'yellow'
> - 'fevver' instead of 'feather'.

Stammering

Stammering (or stuttering) is another common problem that young children may experience when learning to speak. This usually occurs between the ages of two to four years. Children tend to speak so quickly that they make mistakes and stammer over the words. This is a normal stage that most children go through.

Adults should not put pressure on the child to speak correctly as this may make the problem worse. Instead, they should be patient and give praise and encouragement to a child who is stammering. If, however, the problem continues beyond the age of four or when the child starts school, help may be needed from a speech therapist. A speech therapist specialises in speech problems and is trained to help children to correct their speech.

Deafness

Deafness is linked to poor speech development. It is very important for a child to have regular hearing tests so that any problems with hearing can be identified and treated. A deaf child will be slow to learn to speak or may not be able to speak at all if the deafness is total.

PRE-READING SKILLS

Pre-reading is a term used to describe all the skills a child needs to have acquired before learning to read. Reading is linked to language development, since it encourages and increases the child's vocabulary and grammar.

> **Pre-reading skills include:**
> - being able to match similar objects together, e.g. dominoes, pictures and shape sorting
> - playing games, e.g. snakes and ladders or ludo, that involve counting
> - knowing that symbols represent something, e.g. green traffic light means go
> - understanding the sequence of events, e.g. in a story.

Sorting shapes

Books

Babies and young children can be encouraged to develop pre-reading skills by parents or carers providing books from an early age. First books should have large, colourful pictures of everyday objects to attract the baby's attention. They are usually made of cloth or thick board, as the baby will put them into its mouth and chew them. Books that are waterproof and made of plastic can be used in the bath.

Exploring a picture book

Alphabet or number books are appropriate for a child aged 12 months and older. These will encourage the development of number and letter recognition. Nursery rhyme or song books will encourage a child to join in and learn these rhymes.

'Lift the flap' books, and books that make noises when buttons are pressed, add to the variety of books available. These will add interest and stimulation for the child.

Children of all ages enjoy being read to and parents or carers should include a story in the child's regular bedtime routine to encourage reading as an enjoyable activity when the child gets older.

From around the age of three years, the child will spend a long time looking at books. By now, these books will contain simple stories and a child will know these stories well. At this age, a child's concentration will start to increase and they will be able to tell a story by looking at the pictures.

All these pre-reading skills will help a child when they start school and begin to read for themselves. Children should still be read aloud to and should be continually stimulated by their parents or carers to read. A variety of books should always be available so that the child can select a book for pleasure. Visits to the local library could also be made, especially if there are not many books at home.

PRE-WRITING SKILLS

Before starting school, it will help if the child has acquired some pre-writing skills. These are closely linked to speech development as well as pre-reading skills. It is useful if the child can hold a pencil correctly and perhaps form shapes of letters. Reading books will help develop skills such as learning to spell and using grammar and punctuation correctly. All these skills will develop gradually once the child has started school and parents and carers should continue to offer encouragement.

KEY POINTS

- Speech problems are common and most children pass through this stage without too much difficulty.
- Pre-reading activities are very important to prepare a child for learning to read.
- Parents or carers should offer stimulation by providing a variety of books and by reading stories to their children.

KEY TASKS

1 a At around what age does stammering occur?

  b How can a parent or carer help a child who is stammering?

2 Why is it important that deafness is identified in a young child?

3 a Suggest three pre-reading skills.

  b Explain how a parent or carer can encourage these skills.

4 What is the role of a speech therapist?

FURTHER WORK

Investigate the wide variety of books that are available for children under the age of five. Record your findings in an appropriate way, making use of ICT.

Think about it

Think of an activity that could be used with a child to encourage a pre-reading skill.

Talk about it

- Deaf children cannot hear the spoken word. How does this affect their development?
- Discuss the importance of screening tests on hearing for babies and young children.

Conditions for emotional development

BONDING

The bonding of a baby with the parents or carers in the first days of the baby's life is very important. Bonding means the feelings of love and affection between the parents or carers and the baby.

These feelings develop during the early days after the birth, providing the baby is cuddled closely, and this helps babies develop feelings and emotions towards the people around them. The love given freely by parents or carers is often called unconditional love, meaning that they give that love without any conditions such as whether the child is well behaved or not.

A father bonding with his baby

Bonds of affection between mother and baby

Immediately after birth, the mother is given the baby to cuddle and hold close. Skin and eye contact play an important part in developing strong bonds of affection. Holding the baby close, e.g. at feeding time, will encourage these bonds to develop and help the baby to feel secure and comforted. It is important that the father also develops these bonds of affection and, if he is present at the birth, he will be involved straight away.

ENVIRONMENTAL FACTORS

The environment in which children grow up plays an important part in the way they develop emotionally. This includes the home conditions, the way in which the child is brought up and their life experiences.

The following are conditions necessary for the development of the emotions in a child:

- to receive love and affection from parents or carers and friends around the baby
- given opportunities to be independent
- valued as individuals
- acceptable behaviour encouraged
- reassured and helped to develop confidence
- feelings of security in relationships with others.

If these conditions are met by the parents or carers, the child will feel safe and secure. A child will progress in a positive way if he or she has this security and will have high self-esteem. At times, however, children may still feel insecure and may develop fears about something that is happening in their life. The insecure child may feel unwanted and develop low self-esteem. They may start to behave badly in order to get more attention from parents or carers. They may develop negative emotions such as jealousy, shyness, rudeness and aggression. Usually, a child will overcome many of these insecurities if given plenty of love and attention from parents or carers.

REGRESSION

Some children may regress in their behaviour. Regression means that the child can go backwards in an area of development that he or she has already acquired, e.g. if a child has been dry at night he or she may start to wet the bed again.

The source of the insecurity needs to be identified so that the problem can be dealt with. For example, if the child is feeling worried about starting school and this has caused the regression, as long as the parent or carer deals with this in a calm and patient manner and talks to the child, the problem can be sorted out and the child will, given time, stop wetting the bed again. If the child is constantly shouted at about wetting the bed and is not spoken to or helped with the problem, no improvement will be made.

SIBLING RIVALRY

The term 'sibling' means a brother or a sister. **Sibling rivalry** means that the child may feel left out because a brother or sister is getting more attention. This can be very common when a new baby is born in the family. Obviously, the baby will be getting a lot of attention and the sibling may feel excluded. This may lead to feelings of jealousy towards the new baby.

A jealous older sibling may express these feelings by:

- becoming clingy towards the parents or carers
- hitting out at someone
- pinching
- taking toys away from others
- becoming withdrawn
- regressing in behaviour.

Parents or carers need to be aware of these feelings and should:

- involve the child with the coming birth of the baby
- encourage the child to help choose items for the baby
- offer plenty of affection
- talk to the child about the baby
- say how important the child is within the family
- encourage the child to help with the baby when it arrives.

These strategies will help the child to feel secure and overcome their feelings of jealousy.

FEARS AND NIGHTMARES

Children may develop fears that are very real to them, e.g. of the dark, animals, insects and noises. A child's imagination starts to develop at around the age of two years and it is this development, linked with a lack of understanding, that causes these fears. Nightmares may be a result of these fears, and a child who has nightmares regularly must be comforted and reassured. Sometimes they are linked with a major life event such as starting school or unhappiness in the home. Nightmares usually stop once the cause has been dealt with.

COMFORTERS

Many children have a comforter such as a favourite soft toy, a piece of cloth or a blanket, which they adopt themselves. These offer security to the child, especially at night, and the child becomes very attached to the comforter. Children will grow out of these comforters in time, but may need them for several years.

KEY POINTS

- It is important that bonding is developed in the first days of a baby's life in order to establish feelings of love and affection between the parents or carers and the baby.
- Parents or carers should meet several conditions of emotional development in order for the child to feel safe and secure.
- A child who feels insecure may have negative feelings and these may be shown in a variety of ways.

KEY TASKS

1 What is meant by the term 'bonding'?
2 Suggest six conditions of emotional development.
3 a Explain the following terms:
   i Regression ii Sibling rivalry.
  b How should a parent or carer react to each situation?
4 Explain the meaning of the term 'bonds of attachment'.
5 Describe how having high self-esteem benefits a child.

Think about it

What sort of fears do you think a two and a half year old child is likely to have?

Stages of emotional development

Emotional development is the development of a child's emotions. Children need to learn how to control their emotions in order to be accepted within the community in which they live. Emotional development is linked with other areas, but particularly with social development.

LINK For more information on social development see pages 122–123.

Emotions and socialisation are closely linked, as children need to feel secure and loved in order to develop their own personality in a way that is acceptable in society.

POSITIVE AND NEGATIVE EMOTIONS

Everyone experiences both positive and negative emotions and these feelings can often get mixed up. Positive emotions, e.g. happiness, joy, pleasure, love and excitement, need to be encouraged. Negative emotions, e.g. anger, guilt, hate, jealousy and impatience, should be controlled. All these emotions are going to be felt at some time and the child needs to learn how to control these feelings.

Parents or carers should be aware that children should be allowed to express these emotions through play (e.g. role-play) so that they can experience positive and negative feelings. Parents or carers should provide opportunities for their child to play in this way, as it will encourage them to develop personality and independence.

THE CHILD'S PERSONALITY

The child's personality develops gradually over a long period of time – up to five years. Babies and young children under the age of two years think that they are the most important person, and that everything and everybody revolves around them. After the age of two years, children begin to respond to those around them. They start to care for younger children and show some understanding towards the needs of others.

The way in which children develop emotionally depends on their character, the genes they have inherited and the way they feel about themselves. The influence of friends, family and the environment all help to shape a child's personality.

STAGES OF EMOTIONAL DEVELOPMENT

As with other areas of development, a child passes through different stages. The milestones that are shown below are given for the average age only as each child develops at a different pace.

> **These milestones are referred to as 'norms':**
>
> - newborn babies use body movements to express pleasure, e.g. when being fed
> - at one month, the baby begins to show some personality, e.g. calm or excitable
> - by three months, the baby enjoys company and routines, e.g. bathtime

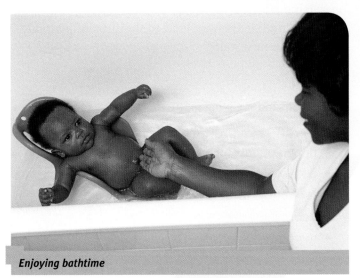

Enjoying bathtime

> - at around six months, the baby may develop shyness and becomes upset when its mother leaves the room
> - at nine months, the baby expresses negative emotions, e.g. anger, may use a comfort toy, develops a fear of strangers and develops likes and dislikes, e.g. food at mealtimes
> - by 12 months, the baby seeks attention and reassurance from adults and shows affection to familiar people
> - by 15 months, the child begins to co-operate with others but may also begin to have temper tantrums. The child's moods may swing from a positive to a negative emotion fairly rapidly

- at 18 months, the child develops more independence, expresses rage and frustration and shows strong emotions

- at the age of five years, the child shows sympathy to others who are hurt, has very definite likes and dislikes and may be happy to leave parents or carers for a while, e.g. to go to school.

A temper tantrum

- at around two years, temper tantrums may be more frequent and the child may become more curious about its environment
- at two and a half years, the child may have fears about the surroundings or people they are familiar with for no reason, e.g. fear of the dark
- by the age of three years, the child begins to care for a younger child, independence is developing further and the child becomes more stable and emotionally secure

Caring for a younger child

- by four years old, the child may develop a sense of humour, expresses many emotions through 'pretend' or imaginative play and will be strongly self-willed

KEY POINTS

- Emotional development is linked to all areas of development, but especially socialisation.
- There are many feelings experienced by a child and parents or carers should provide opportunities in play for the child to be able to express these feelings.
- There are several stages of emotional development that a child passes through.
- A child's personality will depend on the genes inherited and the influence of everyone around them.

KEY TASKS

1 What do you understand by the term 'emotional development'?

2 List four positive and four negative emotions.

3 Suggest two factors that influence a child's personality.

4 Give the average age for the following emotional development milestones:

  a Becomes upset when their mother leaves.

  b Shows affection to familiar people.

  c Has frequent temper tantrums.

  d Develops a sense of humour.

5 Explain what is meant by the term 'the terrible twos'.

FURTHER WORK

Observe and record any emotions a child may demonstrate during activities that may be taking place, e.g. at mealtimes, bathtimes or an organised play session.

GradeStudio

These are examples of the types of question you may meet in the exam:

1 There are many reasons why a two-year-old child may have a temper tantrum. Suggest three.

2 Name three ways a temper tantrum should be dealt with by a parent or carer.

Social development

Social development is the process of children learning how to behave and how to fit in with the people around them. A child needs to develop skills and attitudes that are seen to be acceptable within the community in which he or she lives. Socialisation means learning the social skills that enable a child to get on with others and to behave in a way that is acceptable to others.

Parents or carers should encourage a child in the development of their social skills by:

- providing a loving, secure home
- encouraging opportunities for playing
- taking the child out on visits
- encouraging the child to share
- setting a good example on how to behave
- giving firm, fair discipline
- communicating with the child, e.g. at mealtimes
- reinforcing acceptable behaviour, e.g. manners, washing hands before mealtimes.

STAGES OF SOCIAL DEVELOPMENT

As with all areas of development, there are milestones or norms in social development that all children pass through.

These milestones in social development include:

- newborn babies cry if they are lonely and can be comforted when they are cuddled
- at around one month, babies can recognise their mother's face and will begin to smile in response to another adult
- by three months, the baby enjoys other people's company, smiles when spoken to and enjoys feeding time
- by six months, a baby offers toys to others, may be shy and wary of strangers and manages to feed itself using its fingers
- at around nine months, the baby smiles at a mirror, holds a spoon and drinks from a cup, plays alone for a while and enjoys peek-a-boo games
- at 12 months old, the baby helps with feeding and dressing, enjoys hugging a familiar person and joins in conversations at mealtimes

Playing alone

- at 15 months, the child has developed self-confidence and copies others. Simple household tasks are enjoyed, e.g. dusting
- by the age of 18 months, the child continues to play alone, is keen to dress themselves, can hold a cup and feed themselves quite well. The child is slowly becoming more independent in some skills
- at two years of age, the child may be independent sometimes but at other times may be dependent and cling to a familiar person. They will eat independently and call themselves by their own name
- at around two and a half years of age, the child is involved in **parallel play**, goes to the toilet independently (but may need some help with their clothing) and is competent with a spoon and perhaps a fork
- by the age of three years, the child may be dry

Showing independence

at night, can do some dressing and undressing, enjoys pretend play and family mealtimes, helps adults to tidy up, takes part in **joining-in play** and makes friends

- at around the age of four years, the child becomes involved in **co-operative play**, can wash and dry hands, cleans teeth, undresses and dresses (except for laces and fastenings at the back)

- by five years of age, the child chooses his or her own friends, comforts others if they are upset, eats correctly, enjoys caring for animals and knows his or her full name and address. A child of this age can keep themselves occupied for a long time by looking at a book or DVD.

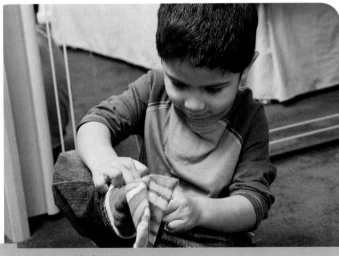
Dressing unaided

Children are not born with these social skills – they have to learn them. It is therefore the parents' or carers' responsibility to teach these skills if the child is to behave in an acceptable way in society.

THE INFLUENCE OF THE ENVIRONMENT

A child's environment can influence the way their social skills develop. If the child lives in a remote country area, it may be difficult to have contact with others of the same age, or if the child comes from a well-off family, they may have everything they want and may not want to share their possessions. A child from a less well-off family may be jealous of others who have more possessions than them.

The size of the family can also influence the child's social development. A child living in a large family will learn the social skill of sharing with others, but may experience the disadvantages of having less adult attention. An only child will have the advantage

of adult attention, but will not have the opportunities within the family of sharing and playing.

Whatever the environment in which a child grows up, it is the responsibility of the parents or carers to provide the child with as many different opportunities as possible so the child can develop a wide range of social skills. Parents or carers should show children that they are loved constantly, regardless of behaviour, and must provide a stable, secure home where children can feel safe and know that they are supported and encouraged.

🔑 KEY POINTS

- Social development is about learning how to behave in an acceptable way.
- Children have to learn social skills from the people around them – they are not born with this knowledge.
- Parents or carers should encourage and stimulate a child's social skills.
- The environment, financial position and size of the family all have an influence on the way the child develops their social skills.

🔑 KEY TASKS

1 Suggest six ways a parent or carer can encourage a child in developing their social skills.

2 Give an average age for the following stages of social development:
   a May be wary of strangers.
   b Enjoys hugging a familiar person.
   c Copies others.
   d Becomes more independent.
   e Can dress and undress apart from any shoelaces.

3 Explain how the following can influence a child's social skills.
   a The environment.
   b The family's financial position.
   c The size of the family.

4 💡 Suggest three social skills that a child must learn in order to behave in a way that is acceptable to others.

Think about it

When you see children in a variety of situations, note any social skills or lack of them that you may notice.

Social play

Learning to play with other children is an important part of social development. There are several stages of social play and as a child goes through each one they learn how to communicate and get on with other children.

STAGES OF PLAY

Solitary play

Solitary play means playing alone. Babies and young children spend a long time quite happily playing on their own with toys, or carrying out activities.

Parallel play

In parallel play, the child is gaining in confidence and is happy to play beside another child. The children may be doing the same activity, but will not play together yet.

Looking-on play

Looking-on play involves a child watching other children play. The child still plays alone, but is a spectator of play and watches from the edge of a group without playing.

Joining-in play

In this type of play, a child joins in with another child or group of children and does the same activity as all the children but in his or her own way.

Co-operative play

Co-operative play is when children play together, either with another child or in a group. In this play, the children are sharing activities and communicating with each other, e.g. playing a game of football or making biscuits.

SOCIAL BEHAVIOUR

Parents or carers must encourage children to behave in an acceptable manner in order for them to get on with others. Children should be praised when they have shown correct social behaviour, e.g. saying 'please' and 'thank you', taking turns and helping others. If children are encouraged and praised whenever they behave in a socially acceptable way, they will be eager to do it again.

NEGATIVE BEHAVIOUR

Children are naturally not going to behave well all the time.

It is normal for children to be naughty and this can be shown in the following ways:

- temper tantrums
- lying
- aggression towards others
- attention-seeking behaviour.

Temper tantrums

Temper tantrums usually occur between the ages of two and three years and are brought on because the child becomes frustrated. The child should be left until they have calmed down. The child can then be reasoned with and needs to be shown that this behaviour is not acceptable.

Lying

Lying is a common form of unacceptable behaviour. A young child does not know the difference between pretend play and real life at times and this is where the confusion can occur. The parent or carer needs to understand this and help the child to become aware of the difference between truths and lies.

Aggression towards others

Aggression towards others can be in the form of kicking, biting, shouting, and so on. A parent or carer needs to be patient and their careful handling of the situation should ensure that the child settles into a more acceptable way of behaving.

Attention-seeking behaviour

Attention-seeking is common in children between the ages of one and four years. Children like to be the centre of attention. If they achieve this by behaving in a certain way, which goes unchecked by their parents or carers, it will become a habit.

Examples of attention-seeking include:

- refusing to eat
- holding their breath
- refusing to use the toilet
- screaming.

If the parent or carer ignores this behaviour, children will learn that they are not getting the attention that they want and will stop.

A child's personality plays a part in how they behave, e.g. a child who is naturally shy will need to be encouraged to be friendly towards others. Children should be encouraged to bring out the positive side of their personalities and to control the negative side.

LINK For more information on the stages of development see pages 54–59.

KEY POINTS

- There are several stages of social play that a child goes through in order to learn how to socialise with others.
- Children need to know that they must learn to behave in a socially acceptable way.

KEY TASKS

1 Describe five types of social play.

2 Suggest four ways a child may show acceptable social behaviour.

3 Describe ways in which a parent or carer should handle situations of unacceptable behaviour.

4 Explain why social play is a good way for children to learn how to get along with others and give examples to support your suggestions.

Think about it

- How do children know what is an acceptable way to play?
- Does it matter if they upset others?

FURTHER WORK

Observe a child's behaviour when they are playing in a group of children. Write down any social or anti-social behaviour that may be demonstrated.

Behaviour and discipline

Children need guidelines to learn how to behave, and this will affect their social and emotional development. A child needs to know how to control his or her feelings (emotional) and how to behave in an acceptable manner (social). Parents or carers play an important role in teaching a child how to behave. Discipline is needed so that a child will learn.

Discipline is often a difficult job, but parents or carers need to:

- set a good example
- be consistent
- praise the child for good behaviour
- avoid confrontation with the child
- divert the child's attention to another activity if the child is behaving in an unacceptable way
- apologise if they (the parents or carers) have behaved badly, e.g. by being short-tempered.

Discipline needs to be fair, firm, consistent and understood by the child. Children benefit from discipline in the following ways:

- it helps them learn self-control
- it helps them behave in an acceptable way
- it makes them feel secure and safe because they know there are boundaries.

LEVELS OF DISCIPLINE

Too much discipline or not enough can both be harmful to a child and will not help the child learn how to behave.

Too much discipline may:

- cause the child to be miserable
- put too many expectations on the child
- harm the relationship between the child and the parent or carer as it means the parent or carer is constantly telling the child off.

The child who is disciplined too much may be expected to be good all the time and is constantly being told 'don't do that, do this'. Children may feel that they cannot do anything right, which may result in them doing nothing because they are frightened of being told off.

On the other hand, not enough discipline may:

- cause the child to feel insecure
- encourage the child to be rude and selfish
- encourage disobedience in the child.

An undisciplined child will become spoilt, unruly and will have no thought for others. He or she will expect to get everything they want, and may feel insecure as there are no boundaries on behaviour. The child will be at risk from accidents as they will be unaware of dangers.

AT WHAT AGE CAN DISCIPLINE BEGIN?

Discipline can only start when children can understand what is expected of them. By the age of one year, a child will understand the word 'no' and so will begin to be aware of what he or she can and cannot do. After this age, as the child grows older and has greater understanding, he or she will gradually become aware of what is expected.

PRAISE OR PUNISHMENT?

Discipline involves both praise and punishment. A child who has behaved well must be rewarded so that he or she understands what is expected and to encourage further good behaviour. Verbal praise is the most effective way of rewarding a child but, for something special, a parent or carer may offer a present as a means of praise.

Distracting the child with a suitable activity

If a child has behaved badly, he or she needs to be made aware that this is not acceptable. Punishment cannot be given unless the child understands, so a child under one year of age should not be punished as this will cause confusion. However, if a baby of this age is doing something that is not acceptable, e.g. emptying the soil from a house plant, the parent or carer should remove the plant or distract the child with an acceptable activity such as drawing.

PUNISHMENT

Some types of punishment are more appropriate for young children than others.

Here are some ways a parent or carer may discipline a child over the age of one year:

- by showing they are not pleased with the child's behaviour, e.g. by ignoring the child for a while or by putting the child to sit in the corner

- by explaining, for example, why the hot cup should not be touched – if the child can be reasoned with

- by withdrawing the activity or item that caused the problem, e.g. if the child has been scribbling on a wall or chair, remove the pens or crayons for a set time.

Whatever punishment is dealt out to a child, it should be effective and happen straight away. A parent or carer should never say, 'Wait until daddy or mummy comes home' – by the time this happens the child will have forgotten what they are being punished for. Parents or carers should never threaten punishment unless they intend to carry it out. If a child is told, 'Eat your dinner or you won't get any sweets', and is then given the sweets anyway, they will never learn to be obedient.

It is not necessary to smack a child in order to teach a child how to behave. A child who is regularly smacked may, in turn, smack or hit others.

🔑 KEY POINTS

- Discipline is required in order for a child to learn how to behave and how to control his or her feelings.
- Parents or carers should ensure that discipline is fair, firm and that the child understands what is expected of them.
- A child will suffer if there is too much or not enough discipline.
- Children should be given praise for good behaviour and some form of punishment for bad behaviour.
- Punishment should be carried out immediately, but smacking is not necessary as a method of punishment.

🔑 KEY TASKS

1 Why do children need to be disciplined?
2 Suggest six ways in which a parent or carer can help to discipline a child.
3 What are the effects of the following?
   a Too much discipline.   b Not enough discipline.
4 💡 If a child misbehaves constantly, what effects does this have on those around them?
5 💡 Explain what is meant if a child's behaviour is described as 'socially unacceptable'.

Talk about it

Discuss whether you think smacking children is right or wrong.

Think about it

How would you discipline a child?

Children aged about two can be reasoned with

Scribbling on a wall is unacceptable behaviour

Learning through play

All children play, and this is a natural way of learning about and discovering everything around them. Children's play usually goes through various stages, as follows:

solitary	0–2 years	child plays with toy alone
parallel	approximately 2 years	child plays alongside, but not with, another child
looking-on	approximately 3 years	child watches others but does not join in
co-operative	approximately 3–4 years	children play together

Play is important as it encourages all the areas of development – social, physical, intellectual, emotional and language. There are several types of play.

PHYSICAL PLAY

Physical play encourages the development of gross motor skills and fine manipulative skills. Physical play is to do with physical activities, e.g. running, climbing, playing with a ball, and helps the child with body co-ordination.

IMAGINATIVE PLAY

By the age of two years, a child has begun to develop an imagination. It is at this age that **imaginative play** becomes part of a child's learning process. **Role-play** or 'pretend play' helps children to understand the world around them. Dressing-up clothes encourage the child to act out adult roles, e.g. doctors, nurses and teachers, which helps with their emotional development.

Items such as cardboard boxes and reading and listening to stories will also develop the imagination.

CREATIVE PLAY

Creative play is to do with a child expressing their feelings through playing with a variety of materials. Playing with dough, painting, colouring, making music, and building/construction toys are all examples of types of creative play. This type of play encourages the development of physical and intellectual skills.

EXPLORATORY PLAY

Exploratory play involves the senses of sight, touch, smell, taste and hearing – this is known as **sensory exploration**. Babies explore their fingers to begin with and then any object that they can reach. All the senses are used as these objects are held, sucked, smelled, looked at and, if they make a noise, listened to. Exploratory play enables children to find things out for themselves at their own pace. Mathematical and scientific concepts, shapes,

colours, textures, weight and volume are all learned through exploratory play.

MANIPULATIVE PLAY

Manipulative play is to do with the movement of the hands. This encourages physical development and hand–eye co-ordination. Babies play with rattles, activity centres, and so on. For the older child, sewing cards, threading beads, dot-to-dot and drawing all stimulate manipulative play.

SOCIAL PLAY

Social play is to do with the way children play together. This type of play encourages the social development of a child. Sharing and being co-operative within a group teaches acceptable social behaviour.

LINK For more information on social development see pages 122–123.

LINKING THE TYPES OF PLAY

All these types of play are linked together. During a play activity, the child may be using more than one type, e.g. playing a game of pirates with a group of children will involve social, imaginative and physical play.

Apart from encouraging the development areas, play also:

- prevents boredom
- reduces stress
- diverts aggression
- helps towards happiness
- helps children to find out about the world around them.

KEY POINTS

- Play is very important to all children so that they can learn and gain information.
- Play helps to stimulate children's senses and promotes developmental progress in all areas.
- There are several types of play and these provide the child with a variety of activities and skills.

KEY TASKS

1 Explain the meaning of six types of play, giving an example for each one.
2 Name four benefits of play.
3 Why is role-play important to a child? Give four examples of role-play activities or situations.
4 Discuss the importance of a baby being given a toy with a variety of fastenings.

FURTHER WORK

Observe groups of children playing together and record your findings. (This would be an excellent activity to do prior to starting the Child Study Activity.)

Talk about it

Discuss in small groups and then present your findings:

- What was the game you enjoyed most as a child?
- Which skill(s) did it develop?

Selection of toys

Children can play with a variety of household objects and get enjoyment and stimulation from them because they treat them as toys. However, there is also a wide range of toys on the market that are specially made to help a child learn.

If toys are to be successful they should:

- be suitable for the age of the child
- be strong enough
- be suitable for the ability of the child
- be made of safe materials
- be made to help develop new skills
- have some appeal to the child
- be made to last a long time.

SAFETY OF TOYS

All toys must be safe for the child to play with and should be made to meet certain safety standards.

The following are toy safety points:

- there should be no sharp edges
- there should be no loose parts, e.g. eyes on dolls or teddy bears
- painted toys should be lead-free
- they should have a safety mark, e.g. the CE 'lion' mark
- they should be strong so that they do not break easily
- they should be free from staples and spikes.

All toys given to children should contain these safety symbols

It is also useful for toys to be washable so that they can be kept clean. This is especially important for a young baby.

Baby toys develop manipulative skills

TOYS FOR DIFFERENT AGES AND STAGES OF DEVELOPMENT

Up to the age of six months, a baby is developing sensory skills such as listening, grasping, reaching out, eye movements and exploring. Suitable toys for this age would be rattles, mobiles, musical toys, soft toys and plastic keys.

Between the ages of six and 12 months, the baby's manipulative skills are developing, as well as hand–eye co-ordination. Sensory skills are developing further, and sitting and crawling skills are also developing. Suitable toys would be push-and-pull-along toys, activity centres, building bricks and stacking beakers.

Around the age of 12 to 18 months, the child is developing balance and walking skills, can control hand movements with some accuracy and is developing language skills. Toys such as shape sorters, picture books, pop-up toys, sand and water and construction toys are ideal.

At 18 months to two years, a child is running and climbing. Hand–eye co-ordination skills are developing further and the child is learning these skills rapidly. Suitable toys would be large jigsaws, a ball, toys with moving parts and nursery rhyme and story books.

By the age of two to three years, a child is very curious and fine manipulative skills are more developed. Gross motor skills are also improving and the child can recognise some colours and size. Suitable toys would be picture dominoes, pencils, paints, threading beads and a tricycle.

At three to four years the child has good gross motor skills, e.g. hopping and skipping, enjoys pretend play and begins to understand mathematical

Young children enjoy painting

the child is older, he or she will learn to stack them, talk about colours, count them in number games and learn about size. The child also develops the concept of filling and emptying the beakers when playing with sand and water. The beakers can encourage social skills when playing with a group of children. When stacking the beakers, an outlet for aggression would be to knock them over, therefore expressing their emotions. All the areas of development are covered by this simple toy across the age ranges, including social, intellectual, physical, emotional and language skills.

concepts. Suitable toys would be a bike with stabilisers, dressing-up clothes, modelling dough, a climbing frame and constructional toys.

By the age of four to five years, the child has a longer concentration span and precise hand–eye co-ordination. Balance and fine manipulative skills are well developed and the imagination is developing. Suitable toys would include counting games, a clock, a pretend shop, alphabet games, weighing and measuring activities and objects useful for baking and gardening.

Dressing up

ADAPTABILITY OF TOYS

Many toys are appropriate to children from one year right through to the age of five. They encourage a variety of different skills over the years and provide interest for the child during that time. An example of such a toy would be stacking beakers.

These are appropriate from the age of six to 12 months, when the baby can grasp a beaker. When

KEY POINTS

- In order for toys to be successful, they should be interesting and attractive as well as strong, safe and suitable for the child.
- The safety of a toy is of the utmost importance and several points should be looked for when buying a toy.
- There are many toys available that cover all the areas of development and these will stimulate and encourage these skills.
- Toys that have been bought wisely and carefully should last a long time throughout childhood.

KEY TASKS

1 Give seven points to look for when buying toys.
2 List five safety points to consider.
3 Suggest toys or activities for the following age groups.
   a Up to six months.
   b Between twelve and eighteen months.
   c Two to three years.
   d Four to five years.
4 Which features make a toy interesting and attractive?
5 Explain how a toy might last a child from babyhood to five years of age.

FOR FURTHER REFERENCE
For more information on suitable toys look at the Early Learning Centre catalogue or visit its website via our hotlinks website.

Think about it

Why do you think some children get really attached to a particular toy?

I really find that writing things down is the best way for me to remember information that I need to know for the exam, especially on the developing skills section.

For example the meaning of each of these development terms:

• Physical   • Social   • Emotional   • Intellectual

And then 'what is meant by a stimulating environment?' or 'how do children learn through play?'.

If I go through each of these points in my original notes and write out the answers I find that I can read them over and over again when revising.

Lakshmi

I found that an interesting way of revising the work we did on behaviour was to read the passage and create a chart containing the most important points to revise. The passage of information read:

Jade is three and a half years old and has many toys. Her father, Tom, is trying to teach her to pick up her toys and put them away tidily. She refuses to do this. She sometimes throws her toys across the room or breaks them by jumping on them. Jade has also scribbled on the wall using felt tip pens, which she thinks is funny. Tom does not know how to discipline Jade. He very often gives in to her and lets her do what she likes.

I compiled a chart to organise the important points to revise.

Jade

Reasons why Stephanie is so naughty	Advice for Tom on disciplining Stephanie
Tom is not consistent: • sometimes he is firm • sometimes he is lenient.	Be consistent in his approach. Always discipline Stephanie in the same way when she is naughty.
She has no rules to follow.	Decide on rules and stick to them **every time**.
She does not understand that breaking things is wrong.	Explain right from wrong.
Breaking things gains attention.	If she breaks things remove them and totally ignore her.
Laughing when she is naughty gets her attention.	When she laughs, do not respond to her. Remove the pens then ignore her.
She is not always made to do what she is asked.	Reward her when she does as she is asked and give lots of praise when she behaves well.

Add more suggestions of your own if you can.

I really enjoyed the session where we revised play. I like discussion lessons and got lots of useful points from this one. We discussed the statement below and it really helped me to remember the points we talked about:

'Children can express themselves through play both emotionally and intellectually.'

Chantelle

Unit 5 revision checklist: intellectual, social and emotional development		
Language development	• Verbal and non-verbal communication skills • Speech problems • Listening and understanding • Stages of development	❑ ❑ ❑ ❑
Social development	• Taking turns • Mixing with others • Sharing skills • Able to interact and be friendly • Manners, including table manners	❑ ❑ ❑ ❑ ❑
Emotional development	• Showing feelings, e.g. happiness • Being loving and caring • Being friendly • Security	❑ ❑ ❑ ❑

Tests!

A really good way to help with revision is to test yourself and your friends. It really helps to work together. . . You could create some questions to answer together!

Exam**Café**

Sample question

The following is an example of a fairly brief question on children's books. This type of question is called an open-ended question, which means that there is a wide range of information that could go into the answer.

> How do books play an important part in a child's development? **(10 marks)**

Examiner tips

Although the question is short the answer is not – so don't be fooled into writing a very brief explanation worth very few marks.

Your answer here must explain very clearly all the benefits that books offer a child. Your plan could include the following points:

- for entertainment value
- encourages an interest in a topic or subject
- develops a love of, and encourages, reading
- improves knowledge
- gives pleasure
- increases language and understanding.

And of course there are many more for you to find to develop a good-quality answer.

Here's another essay-style question on discipline:

> In order to learn acceptable ways to behave children need good discipline.
> - Suggest some suitable methods to teach a child good discipline.
> - Explain why it is important for children to learn acceptable patterns of behaviour. **(total 15 marks)**

Examiner tips

This is another question requiring a detailed or essay-style answer. Remember that you must spend approximately the same amount of time on each part and achieve a similar quality in both parts of your answer to get high marks.

It's always a good idea to make a plan to help you to organise your answers.

You can do this by drawing out a spidergram for each part or by creating a set of bullet points for each section. Do whatever is most helpful for you.

When you actually start to write out your answer be sure to explain each part thoroughly. Whenever possible give a reason. For example, when you make a statement go on to say 'The reason for this is. . . or 'This is due to. . . or 'This can be explained by. . . '

Whenever you can, you should give an example as this helps the examiner to understand the meaning of your answer and demonstrates your knowledge and understanding of the subject.

By doing this you will be writing a more detailed answer and it will help you express what you are trying to say more clearly.

An example of a short answer question:

Give three ways play can benefit a child.   **(3 marks)**

Examiner tips

Remember:
- if there are three marks in the brackets you need to give three different points
- do not jot down odd words – explain your point properly
- never leave an answer out – guess if you have to but never leave a blank space as you can be sure to score zero for that!

Key words	
cognitive	the development of understanding, reasoning and learning
concepts	general ideas about life, such as heat, time and light
co-operative play	playing in a group
creative play	the expression of feelings through materials, e.g. painting
exploratory play	involves the senses, such as touching different textures on a play mat
imaginative play	using the imagination through play, for example playing shops
joining-in play	joining in with other children and doing the same activity but the child's own way
looking-on play	watching other children play
manipulative play	the movement of the hands, for example threading beads
mispronunciations	mistakes made when learning to pronounce words
nature	refers to the child's natural ability
nurture	the way the child is stimulated and interacted with
parallel play	playing alongside another child, but not playing together
physical play	physical activities, for example running and climbing
pre-reading	the skills the child needs to have acquired before learning to read
role-play	acting out adult roles, for example doctors and nurses
sibling rivalry	competition between brothers and sisters
social play	the way children play together, for example playing football
solitary play	playing alone

Daycare provision

Over the last 25 years, the need for daycare provision has increased. This is because:

- many families have one or both parents or carers working and need to find other carers for their children during the day
- it is recognised that children benefit from early years experiences before they start formal school
- the child may have special needs and require special provision to enable them to make progress.

Many working parents or carers use some formal childcare arrangements, whereas other parents or carers use informal support such as family and friends. A quarter of all three- and four-year-olds receive some type of pre-school or nursery education.

The Early Years Foundation Stage

The Early Years Foundation Stage (EYFS), which came into force in September 2008, is the new regulatory and quality framework for the provision of learning, development and care for children between birth and the academic year in which they turn five (0–5).

From September 2008, all providers of child care will be inspected by Ofsted inspectors.

There is a wide range of daycare provision available to children under five years of age including day nurseries and workplace crèches, nursery schools, childminders and playgroups.

DAY NURSERIES

Day nurseries offer a range of care where children are looked after during their parents' or carers' working hours. Some are run by the local authority, others by the employer or educational institute and some are run privately. All day nurseries need to be registered and must follow government guidelines about staffing, facilities, safety and other practical issues.

> **Day nurseries are widely used because they:**
> - provide children with good, basic care to standards which are clearly laid down
> - operate hours to suit the needs of working parents or carers
> - give children opportunities for socialisation with other children in a structured environment
> - provide a wide range of resources, activities and learning opportunities.

Workplace crèches

Workplace crèches are a form of day nursery provision provided to meet the needs of the workforce. They are often on the employer's premises and run to the same standards as other nurseries.

NURSERY SCHOOLS

Nursery schools are different from day nurseries as they provide a more formal educational setting. Government policy has been to increase the number of children attending nursery schools. Most local authorities offer some nursery school provision for children under the age of five, and it is also available privately. Nursery schools are subject to regulation and inspection to make sure the guidelines that are laid down for them are followed.

CHILDMINDERS

Childminders provide a care service for young children in a home environment, looking after only

A childminder is a popular form of daycare

a few children at a time. Most childminders look after up to six young children, including any of their own. They are required to be registered and to meet certain standards.

Parents or carers might choose a childminder because:

- the hours can often be more flexible to suit the needs of working parents
- the home environment may be seen as more appropriate and less threatening for the very young child
- it is sometimes a cheaper form of childcare provision
- the child may be with other young children in a family environment.

PLAYGROUPS

Playgroups are usually held in local premises, such as village halls, for morning sessions only during school term time. They are for children aged between three and five years old, who usually attend for two or three mornings a week. Playgroups are managed by qualified staff who are specially trained to work with children of this age.

Playgroups are often referred to as pre-schools. Until recently they were the most popular form of pre-school provision but the number of children attending playgroups has decreased.

Numbers attending playgroups may be falling because:

- more women are working and need full-time daycare provision for their children, which the playgroup cannot provide
- there is an increasing provision for pre-school education in nursery school places in local primary schools.

Playgroups are recognised as part of the pre-school education provision for the under fives. The child has the opportunity to learn through play in a wide range of activities from water play to imaginative play. Playgroups are inspected to assess the value of the education provided.

FLEXIBLE WORK PRACTICES

Many employers have developed new initiatives to meet the needs of working parents. These practices give parents and carers more flexibility in their childcare arrangements.

Flexible work practices may include:

- job sharing – a practice where two people share one job and one salary to enable them to have the benefits of continuing employment, but to have time with their children while they are growing up
- flexible hours – this enables parents and carers to fit their working day around their childcare arrangements, e.g. they start earlier and finish earlier
- working from home – with modern communication systems this is becoming a popular option for some parents and carers.

KEY POINTS

- **Many working parents or carers rely on some form of childcare.**
- **Day nurseries and workplace crèches offer care for children while parents or carers are at work.**
- **Nursery schools provide a more formal educational setting.**
- **Playgroups are usually local, part-time settings for children under the age of five.**

KEY TASKS

1 **Explain why there is an increase in the need for daycare provision.**
2 **What is the meaning of the term 'childminder'?**
3 **Why do many parents and carers choose to use a childminder? What should they consider when choosing a childminder?**
4 **Compare and contrast the different types of daycare provision available.**

FURTHER WORK

Carry out a survey in your local area to find out what daycare provision is available. Present your results as a report.

Think about it

Should parents feel guilty about someone else looking after their children?

The community

A community is a group of people living in a local area. The needs of communities in the UK are met by local authorities and other government agencies such as the National Health Service. These agencies have a statutory duty, which means they are directed by law to look after the needs of individuals and families in the community.

Services provided for the community include:

- meeting the personal needs of the family for housing, education and health
- providing community facilities in the local area such as parks, sports centres and libraries
- protecting the family by the provision of emergency services (fire, ambulance and police)
- supplying environmental services to include street cleaning, refuse and recycling.

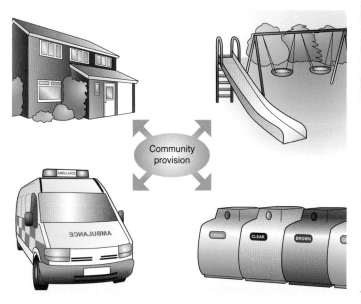

Community provision

STATUTORY SUPPORT FOR FAMILIES

Statutory support is provided for families as part of the **social security system** in the UK. Many families need help and support to provide for their members. The support offered will depend on the particular needs of the family, but it can be practical (such as help in finding appropriate housing), financial (such as receiving benefits) or advisory (such as help in managing a special needs child).

FINANCIAL SUPPORT FOR FAMILIES

A range of benefits and tax credits are available to families, who can get advice and information from their local benefits agency office.

Means testing

For families to receive some types of financial support they are **means tested**. The family's income is compared with a standard amount of money to assess if they need financial support. Means-tested benefits are said to be targeted, which means they are directed at the families most in need.

Means-tested benefits include:

- **Working tax credit**, which supports families on low income but who are in employment and have at least one child
- **income support**, which is a benefit for those whose income falls below a given amount of money, and who are not working or are working fewer than 16 hours a week
- **housing benefit** and **council tax benefit** assist in the costs of housing for families on low incomes
- **Sure Start maternity grants**, which help pay for the costs of a new baby. It is a single payment for families on low income.

Tax credits

Tax credits are payments from the government to help with day-to-day costs for families and young people. Two types of tax credits are available: **child tax credits** and working tax credit.

Child tax credit is a payment to help parents and carers of children aged under 16 or qualifying young people aged under 20. They do not have to be working to claim and it is paid directly to the person responsible for the children. It is made up of a family element, a child element and a disability element.

Working tax credit is for people who are in paid work for at least 16 hours a week, *and* are responsible for at least one child, or are disabled, or are aged 25 and working more than 30 hours a week.

🔍 **FOR FURTHER REFERENCE** For information on tax credits visit the website that can be accessed via our hotlinks website.

Universal benefits

Universal benefits are benefits available to everyone entitled to receive that benefit, regardless of income, such as child benefit. These benefits are targeted at specific groups such as children or the disabled.

Universal benefits include:

- **child benefit** – an allowance paid to a parent or carer of every child. The allowance is paid until the child leaves full-time education or is 18 years of age.
- **disability allowance** – paid to help cover the costs of caring for a disabled child or adult
- free dental treatment and medical prescriptions for all children until they leave full-time education.

Other types of benefit

Type of benefit	Who benefits
Statutory Maternity Pay (SMP)	Pregnant women who have worked for the same employer for six months
Maternity Allowance (MA)	Some pregnant women who may not qualify for SMP
Help with NHS costs	Free dental treatment and prescriptions for women during pregnancy and until the baby is one year old

KEY POINTS

- The community provides a wide range of services for families.
- Information about financial support for families is available at the local benefits agency office.
- Means-tested benefits are targeted at families in greatest need.
- Universal benefits are available to everyone, regardless of income.

KEY TASKS

1 Explain the difference between means-tested and universal benefits.
2 Describe the services that are provided for families in the community.
3 Suggest four sources of help for parents and explain each source.

FURTHER WORK

1 Use a map of your local area to identify where services provided to the community are located.
2 Collect a selection of current benefits agency leaflets from your local post office or benefits agency office. Prepare a short presentation to explain one of the benefits available to families.

Talk about it

Discuss the following question in groups. Then prepare a presentation giving points for and against.

'Should some people receive benefits when other people have to work for everything that they need?'

GradeStudio

This is a possible short answer question:

'A universal benefit is one that is available to all. Name two universal benefits.'   (2 marks)

You could suggest any two of: free prescriptions, free eye tests and glasses, free dental treatment, child benefit, disability allowance.

Voluntary agencies

Other agencies that provide support to families are voluntary organisations. These are non-profit making bodies which are set up to help and support individuals and families.

Voluntary organisations:

- often work with local authorities to provide a mixture of welfare provision
- can help meet the needs of the family when they cannot be met by the statutory services
- can respond quickly in times of urgent or emergency need
- have staff who are committed and have specific experience.

THE ROLE OF VOLUNTARY AGENCIES

Voluntary agencies can help and support families in the community in a number of different ways.

Direct assistance

Direct assistance means giving practical and physical help to children and families in need. The National Society for the Prevention of Cruelty to Children (NSPCC) is an important voluntary organisation that works with the social services to support children and families in a number of different ways. Another example of direct assistance is the provision of soft playroom equipment for children with special needs as part of the Children in Need campaign.

Advice and counselling

Some agencies offer advice and counselling, helping individuals and families in particular situations.

Such advice agencies include:

- Citizens Advice Bureau, which offers help and advice to families about a wide range of issues, from debt management to welfare benefits
- ChildLine, which offers confidential support and advice to children through a free telephone number (0800 1111) and website service
- Parents Anonymous, which offers information, support and help for parents or carers and families.

The Citizens Advice Bureau

The Citizens Advice Bureau (CAB) can help individuals and families by providing information and advice about a range of issues. The information it gives is offered to anyone about any subject, and is:

- independent
- confidential
- impartial
- free.

It provides information about:

- benefits
- civil rights
- consumer affairs
- education
- employment
- family matters health
- housing
- immigration
- legal systems
- tax.

Self-help groups

Individuals and families with the same concerns may work together to support and share problems and set up self-help groups. One Parent Families/Gingerbread is a support organisation for lone-parent families that offers practical help, contact and information.

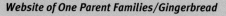

Website of One Parent Families/Gingerbread

Pressure groups

These are voluntary groups set up to actively bring about change. Shelter campaigns on behalf of the homeless and those in poverty without a decent standard of living.

Child Poverty Action Group promotes action for the relief of poverty among children and families.

Non-profit making groups

These groups usually provide a service to the community and although they are often run as a business they do not make a profit – all money generated is used to invest in the service provided. An example is the Women's Royal Voluntary Service (WRVS), which provides a number of services to the community such as the Meals on Wheels service for the elderly and shop facilities at local hospitals.

NATIONAL ASSOCIATION FOR VOLUNTARY AND COMMUNITY ACTION

The National Association for Voluntary and Community Action (NAVCA) works with local voluntary groups and organisations. It plays a key role in trying to match community needs with the voluntary and statutory provision available.

> The role of the NAVCA includes:
> - co-ordinating local voluntary groups such as the WRVS and Citizens Advice Bureau
> - liaising with the local authority social services
> - recruiting and placing volunteers
> - helping to provide resources for voluntary groups
> - sharing information
> - identifying areas of local need
> - acting as a pressure group to lobby for needs of the community.

INFORMAL CARE

'Informal care' is the term used to describe the type of care given by relatives, friends and neighbours to help and support families. A carer is anyone who gives time and energy looking after a friend or relative who is ill or disabled. A very large proportion of community care is provided informally in this way. For example, a family who has a child with Down's syndrome may need extra help, which might be provided by informal carers who are family friends.

KEY POINTS

- Voluntary agencies often work with the statutory services to provide a mixture of care.
- The National Association for Voluntary Action co-ordinates local voluntary groups.
- Informal care is the care given voluntarily by family, friends and neighbours to help and support individuals and families in need.

KEY TASKS

1 Explain the different types of voluntary agencies.
2 How are local voluntary services co-ordinated?
3 What is an informal carer?
4 Identify a voluntary agency that works with children and find out more about its role. Present your findings in the form of a short report.

FOR FURTHER REFERENCE
Most voluntary agencies provide information services on the Internet and any search engine can be used to access this information.

Services for children and families

PERSONAL SOCIAL SERVICES

The personal social services are designed to meet the social needs of vulnerable groups in society such as children and families in need of support. The services are provided by the local authority or voluntary and private organisations. Many social services departments are now called 'Children and young people's services'. Social workers play a key role in the provision of the personal social services. Access to these services is by referral, which means the social services are initially contacted by the local GP, health visitor or a parent or carer themselves.

Social workers deal with many family issues such as:

- parenting problems
- financial problems
- violence in the home
- child protection
- provision of statutory services.

Social workers who operate in the local authority are often referred to as **field social workers**. They have a multi-disciplinary approach, which means they work with government and voluntary organisations to support and help individuals and families to live a normal life in the community. Their work will often include visiting families in their own homes. They refer to the individuals or families they deal with as clients. Activities of a field social worker include:

- signposting – directing the client to specialist help such as a debt counsellor or benefits agency office
- advocacy – meaning that the social worker acts on the behalf of the family (client) to help put across the client's point of view. This could, for example, be in the case of a legal matter that has come to court
- assessment – where social workers are able to identify the needs of individuals or families in order to offer the appropriate support and guidance.

Social workers offer support to families

FOR FURTHER REFERENCE For information on services and benefits visit the government website via our hotlinks website.

THE NEEDS OF THE LONE-PARENT FAMILY

Many lone-parent families are dependent on support from social services departments in the local authority. Field social workers play a key role in assessing the needs of lone-parent families and directing them to suitable resources and advice

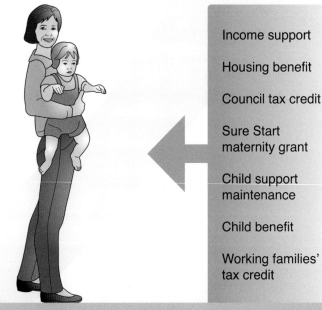

Income support

Housing benefit

Council tax credit

Sure Start maternity grant

Child support maintenance

Child benefit

Working families' tax credit

Benefits that may be available for the lone parent

agencies. Lone-parent families are more likely to have low incomes and to be dependent on social welfare for financial support.

Every Child Matters

Every Child Matters: Change for Children is a government initiative that looks after the well-being of children and young people from birth to 19. The aim is that all children, whatever their background or circumstances, should have the support they need to be healthy, stay safe, enjoy and achieve, make a positive contribution and achieve economic well-being. Organisations involved with providing services to children – such as hospitals, schools, police and voluntary groups – have teamed up to work together in order to protect children and young people from harm and to help them to achieve what they want in life.

TAKE-UP OF BENEFITS

Many families who are entitled to benefits do not apply for them.

Some people may not take up benefits because:

- they do not know what benefits they can get
- the forms may be too difficult and complex for them to complete
- there could be a language barrier, which prevents the family applying for the benefits
- they might be embarrassed about applying for them.

WELFARE-TO-WORK SCHEME

The Welfare-to-Work scheme is a government initiative to encourage people on benefits to find jobs and so become less dependent on welfare provision. Lone parents are one of the groups that are targeted for this programme. The scheme helps with advice, training and re-skilling to open up job opportunities. An important part of the scheme is to give support and financial assistance with childcare. A network of after-school clubs has also been set up to provide supervision and activities until lone parents get back from work.

SURE START

Sure Start is a government programme to provide a range of services to make sure that all children get the best start in life. It aims to help parents by providing information and advice on health and education. Children's centres are being developed across the UK to offer help to parents and children by bringing together childcare, early education, health and family support services for families with children under five years old.

KEY POINTS

- **Lone-parent families often need financial support.**
- **The Welfare-to-Work scheme is an initiative to encourage lone parents to return to work.**
- **The personal social services try to meet the needs of vulnerable families.**
- **Sure Start is an initiative to encourage improved resources for families with children under five.**

KEY TASKS

1 How can the personal social services help meet the needs of vulnerable families?
2 Describe the types of benefits available to lone-parent families.
3 Explain the differences between social security and social services.
4 What is a children's centre?

Children with special needs

A child with special needs requires additional help and support to live a fulfilling life.

A child has special needs if he or she has:

- a disability
- a learning difficulty that leads to greater learning problems than experienced by most children
- their health or development impaired in some way (e.g. if physical development is below average for a child of the same age).

Children with a special need require extra support and care

Children with disabilities share the same basic needs as other children, but the disability or special need may mean they have additional needs.

CONGENITAL DISABILITY

Some disabilities are described as congenital, which means they are present at birth.

Causes of congenital disability can be:

- genetic – where the genetic material inherited from the parents affects the child, e.g. Down's syndrome, haemophilia and **muscular dystrophy**
- brain damage – caused before or during the birth of the baby and often as a result of a lack of oxygen to the baby (this is known as anoxia). **Cerebral palsy** is a congenital condition caused by a lack of oxygen shortly before or during birth
- developmental – where physical development of the foetus is affected during pregnancy. This could be caused by the mother drinking excessive alcohol, smoking or taking drugs. Diseases such as German measles contracted during pregnancy can also lead to failure of development such as cleft palate or deafness.

SPECIFIC DISABILITIES

Physical disability

This is where the disability is related to physical problems such as mobility or co-ordination.

Physical disability can include:

- sensory impairment such as blindness or deafness
- spina bifida – a congenital condition that affects 1 in every 1000 births. The baby is born without a fully formed spine. Surgery can often help children overcome some of the mobility problems
- cerebral palsy – the area of the brain that controls muscle function is damaged at birth. Children with cerebral palsy have difficulty in controlling their fine manipulative and gross motor movements.

Other disabilities include:

- emotional difficulties where children have problems relating to others, such as **autism**
- learning difficulties, which may be a result of a congenital condition such as Down's syndrome
- behavioural problems, where children can be withdrawn, aggressive or hyperactive – this includes conditions such as **attention deficit hyperactivity disorder (ADHD)**.

Children with autism

Children with autism find it difficult to communicate with others, including their families. Autism is four times more likely to occur in boys than girls. Three-quarters of children with autism also have learning difficulties.

Most autistic children have difficulties:

- with speech and language – they are unable to communicate in the usual way, even though they are able to repeat words and phrases
- with social interaction – children with autism find it difficult to form relationships with their peers, and they find it difficult to understand and respond to other children.

Children with Down's syndrome

Down's syndrome is a condition that affects 1 in every 1000 babies born. It occurs in children from all cultural, religious and ethnic groups. It is a genetic condition caused by having an extra chromosome in the body's cells. This chromosome disrupts the development of the cells, producing physical characteristics such as eyes that slant upwards and outwards.

Down's syndrome children also have learning difficulties, which means they have more problems learning than other children of the same age. The chance of having a Down's syndrome child increases with age, particularly if the woman is over the age of 35.

Risk and maternal age – the chance of having a baby with Down's syndrome

Age of mother (years)	Risk
25	1 in 1400
30	1 in 800
35	1 in 380
40	1 in 110
45	1 in 30

EQUAL OPPORTUNITIES AND SPECIAL NEEDS

All children should have equal opportunities and entitlement to learning. Current practice in caring for children with special needs is based on identifying the needs of the individual child, because all children have different needs. A child who is physically immobile may have highly developed intellectual skills but will need help and support with mobility. Physical immobility may slow down the social development of the child, as it limits the child from gaining independence. For some young children with special needs, a little extra support and help is all they need to make progress. Other special needs children may have severe disabilities and need more help and care.

KEY POINTS

- A child with special needs requires help and support to live a fulfilling life.
- A congenital disability is one that is present at birth.
- Down's syndrome is a congenital disability.
- Autistic children find it difficult to communicate with others.
- All children should have equal opportunities to education.

KEY TASKS

1 Explain the term 'special needs'.
2 a What do you call a disability that is present at birth?
  b Name three of these disabilities.
  c What are the causes of these disabilities?
3 Explain the type of support that is available to families with special needs children.
4 What does the term 'equal opportunities' mean?
5 What is the difference between a physical disability and a learning disability?

FOR FURTHER REFERENCE

The Children's Act (1989) encourages the integration of special needs children into mainstream nurseries and schools. This is called inclusive care and education. Go to the website for the Department for Children, Schools and Families via our hotlinks website to find out more.

FURTHER WORK

Find out which voluntary support services are available in your local area for special needs families.

Caring for children with special needs

Families with children with special or additional needs are entitled to a range of statutory benefits and support.

SUPPORT SERVICES

All children have basic needs, and families with special needs children require extra help and support. Local authorities assess these children to identify their needs to make sure help and support are available. Statutory provision for children with special needs and their families includes access to benefits, housing and social services.

Benefits

> **Benefits available to families with special needs children include:**
>
> - Carer's Allowance for carers of children who need constant care
> - Disability Living Allowance for children unable to move around independently
> - financial help with transport to hospital and school.

Housing

Priority in housing is given to families with special needs children. Local authorities often adapt the housing to suit the needs of the child, such as widening doorways for wheelchairs and making entry ramps. Specially designed mobility aids can be provided and fitted in the home.

Social services

Social workers can help and support families to ensure they are aware of the services available to them. This means, for example, giving advice on access to benefits, education, local services and to professionals such as speech therapists.

VOLUNTARY AGENCIES

There are a number of voluntary agencies that support special needs children and their families. Most of these agencies are financed by fundraising, although some receive government help. The Royal Society for Mentally Handicapped Adults and Children (MENCAP) is an example of one of these agencies. It is a national organisation, with branches in most local areas, which raises money to support its work in the community.

> **Voluntary agencies can help special needs families by:**
>
> - giving specialist information
> - offering practical help and support for the families
> - working with the statutory services to make sure families receive help
> - bringing together families of children with similar problems
> - providing **respite care**.

Respite care

Respite care is a support system that enables families with special needs children to have a break from caring for their child. Many voluntary agencies offer respite care.

LEARNING OPPORTUNITIES

The developmental progress of a child with special needs is influenced by the opportunities he or she is given. Progress may be at a different rate to that of other children. Learning programmes that are designed to speed up the development of children with special needs in the pre-school years are known as **early intervention programmes**.

Early intervention programmes can stimulate a child's learning

They can include specific treatments, such as speech therapy and physiotherapy, as well as learning programmes where a trained support worker comes into the home or education setting to work with the child. Many special needs children attend their local school, where a support assistant in the classroom makes sure they have the extra help and support to ensure they make progress.

Opportunity playgroups

Opportunity playgroups are specialist playgroups for children with special needs. They provide learning opportunities to stimulate and challenge the special needs child.

In such playgroups children with special needs can:

- join in some or all of the activities with the help of a carer or support assistant
- receive specialist help and support from trained professionals to help trigger their developmental progress.

TOYS

Toys for children with special needs should be chosen to match the child's stage of development rather than his or her age. For example, a toy that involves posting shapes through holes in a box will suit a child whose hand–eye co-ordination allows them to grasp the object and push it through the hole, regardless of his or her age or ability in other areas of development.

FAMILIES

Most children with special needs live at home with their families. Care of children with special needs presents families with many challenges. The physical care of the child may be very demanding and time consuming resulting in less time or attention for other children in the family. Opportunities for family outings and holidays may be limited. In addition, there may be insensitivity towards the family from others in the community. However, there can also be many positive effects – family bonds become stronger as everyone works to care for and support the child.

ATTITUDES IN SOCIETY

People react in different ways to children with special needs. Some avoid contact because they are embarrassed; others are over-protective. It is important that the lives of all children are valued, and that children with special needs have equal opportunities and enjoy the same rights.

🔑 KEY POINTS

- Families with children who have special needs are entitled to a range of statutory benefits and support.
- Statutory provision for children with special needs and their families includes access to additional benefits, housing and social services.
- Respite care is a support system that enables families with special needs children to have a break from caring for their child.
- Early intervention programmes help speed the developmental progress of the pre-school child with special needs.

🔑 KEY TASKS

1 Explain the range of support services available to families with children with special needs.

2 How can an opportunity playgroup help the development of a child with special needs?

3 💡 Disabilities can delay development. Give two examples of this.

4 💡 Describe the effects of having a child with special needs on the rest of the family.

FURTHER WORK

Identify a charity that works to help and support children with special needs and their families. Find out the range of information and support that it provides.

Talk about it

In groups discuss the types of help that may be needed by a family when looking after a child with special needs. Where can they go to find the help they need?

I always like to put the information from my notes into a chart or table like the one I have started here. That way I find I can remember it more easily. You can do one of your own for any topic.

Junaid

Disorder	Description
Down's syndrome (congenital)	• Caused by an extra chromosome • Eyes tend to slant • Eyelids have extra fold • Learn more slowly
Cystic fibrosis (congenital)	• Affects the lungs • Daily physiotherapy is needed • Affects digestion & absorption of food
Cerebral palsy (congenital)	• Can be caused by lack of oxygen at birth • Difficult to control movement
Spina bifida (congenital)	• Spinal cord damaged • Affects 1 in every 1000 births

Brainstorms are a really good way to remember things.

Millie

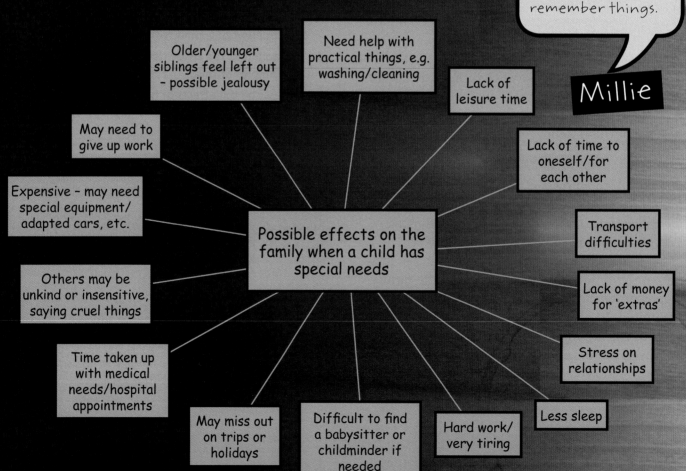

Unit 6 revision checklist: services available to families		
Social services	• Responsibility of the local council/local authority • Provide advice on a wide range of matters (including financial) • Very rarely give money unless in a real emergency situation	❑ ❑ ❑
Social security	• Benefits that come from the government • Financial help for those who need it	❑ ❑
National Health Service (NHS)	• Provide healthcare for all • Not means tested	❑ ❑
Voluntary services/ organisations, e.g. NSPCC; Save the Children; RoSPA	• Independent and rely on the help of volunteers • Not government funded	❑ ❑

Now test yourself!

What do these abbreviations stand for?

RNIB
NSPCC
NAS
CAB
WRVS
CPAG
RNID

Find out any that you don't know.

ExamCafé

Exam preparation

Below is an example of an essay-style question. The idea of including a question of this type on the exam paper is to offer students the chance to show their level of understanding and knowledge to achieve higher level marks.

Examiner tip

It is good advice to do a plan for a question of this type to prevent you from repeating yourself and to keep your focus on the key points of the answer. A spidergram or bullet points are suitable for this.

Tips
A good quick tip is to read the question carefully and to highlight the key words before you go any further.

Understanding exam language

Identify the key words in a question and make sure you understand what they mean:

Describe	means to give the characteristics of something, or a description of it
Explain	means to make something known in detail, giving the meaning as an explanation

Sample essay-style question:

There are many types of support available to benefit the parents and carers of young children.

- Describe the financial benefits that may be available to them.
- Explain the types of support that may be available from social services. **(total 15 marks)**

Examiner tips

When answering a question like this one you need to make sure that you use the correct terminology – which means that you need to have revised thoroughly!

For example, lots of students would use the term 'family allowance' here as a financial benefit, because that is how many people refer to it. The correct term to use is 'child benefit'.

When explaining the types of support available you must not give vague answers like 'advice and support'. You need to explain what types of advice they give and to whom. You need to be very clear on the support that is available, who offers it to whom, and why.

(To help you to be sure of these facts refer back to Unit 6.)

Sample short answer questions:

Sometimes babies are born with congenital disabilities.
i There are many causes of these. Name two. **(2 marks)**
ii Give two examples of congenital disabilities. **(2 marks)**

If a family has a child with special needs they often welcome additional help and support.
i Describe the effects that having this child may have on the family members. **(5 marks)**
ii How could other relatives help and support them? Give three ways. **(3 marks)**

Key words

attention deficit hyperactivity disorder (ADHD)	a disorder characterised by a short attention span and poor concentration
autism	a disorder that affects the ability to communicate with others and form relationships
cerebral palsy	a congenital condition caused by lack of oxygen shortly before or after birth
child benefit	a benefit paid to all parents regardless of income
child tax credit	a payment to help parents and carers who may or may not work
council tax benefit	a benefit that assists in the cost of paying council tax for families on low incomes
disability allowance	an allowance paid to help cover the cost of caring for a disabled child or adult
early intervention programmes	learning programmes designed to speed up the development of children with special needs in the pre-school years
field social workers	social workers who visit individuals and families at home
housing benefit	a benefit that assists in the cost of housing for families on low incomes
income support	a benefit for those whose income falls below a given level of money and are not working, or working fewer than 16 hours a week
means tested	where the income of the family is compared to a standard amount to assess if they are in need of financial support
muscular dystrophy	a genetic muscle disease that causes progressive muscle weakness
opportunity playgroups	specialist playgroups for children with special needs
respite care	a support system that enables families of children with special needs to have a break from caring for their child
social security system	the government support system that provides benefits to those in need
statutory support	support services that have to be provided by the local authority
Sure Start maternity grants	financial support that helps to pay for the costs of a new baby, available as a single payment for families on a low income
universal benefits	benefits available to everyone regardless of income, such as child benefit
working tax credit	a benefit to support families on low income but who are in employment and have at least one child

About the controlled assessment (coursework)

As part of your Child Development for OCR GCSE, you have to complete four pieces of coursework for the internal assessment components. These pieces should consist of:

- one child study task

- three short tasks.

These pieces of coursework count for up to 60 per cent of your final mark. You will also have to sit an exam, which counts for up to 40 per cent of your final mark. You should try to present your coursework using a range of methods, including the use of ICT where appropriate.

Your child study task should take approximately 22 hours to complete and each short task should take approximately 7 hours to complete.

THE CHILD STUDY TASK

This piece of coursework carries 30 per cent of the total marks available. It involves investigation and problem-solving skills, and must include the observation of a child or children.

Before starting this task, it is useful to have already had experience of children and to have spent some time observing them. You should already have covered some of the content of the course before you start your child study task, e.g. physical, social, intellectual and emotional development. Before carrying out your child study task, you should already have done some short tasks to develop your skills of research and investigation.

Selection of the child study task title

The child study task title will be developed during the research section (see pages 153–154). It is vital that you develop and produce your own task title in order to meet the assessment criteria. If you have difficulty achieving this without help, your teacher can offer you support and guidance.

THE SHORT TASKS

The short task titles will be set by OCR. Your teacher will select appropriate tasks from the list provided by OCR. These will be relevant to the subject content you are being taught. The short tasks are pieces of coursework that are short and focused on an area of the subject content. Each short task carries 10 per cent of the total mark available. A number of short tasks may be carried out but only three are selected for the final assessment (30 per cent of the final mark). One will be an investigative task; the other two will be practical tasks.

Selection of the short task titles

The short task titles will be set by your teacher and should be relevant to the subject content being taught. One will be an investigation; the other two will involve some practical work. The amount of time spent on each task will be laid down by your teacher, so you should be aware of how much time you should spend on each area. However, you do not need to record these timings in your short tasks. To conclude, child study and short tasks require a number of skills (see diagram below).

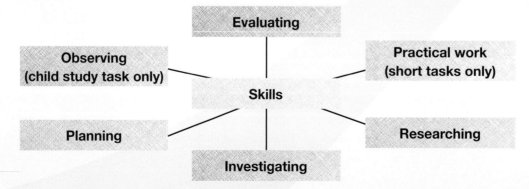

Child study task: research

The child study task includes the following sections:

1 task research

2 selecting and planning the observations

3 practical observations:

  a) observations

  b) applying understanding to observations

4 conclusion and evaluation.

You need to work through each of these sections to produce a good-quality, in-depth piece of coursework.

SECTION 1: TASK RESEARCH

The task research stage involves deciding on a suitable child to study, then finding out about the child and the area(s) of development that you have chosen. It is important that you produce a clear title for your work from the theme you are given.

Choosing a suitable task title

This is where you choose an area of development to study. You must make sure that the area of development is relevant and suitable for the age range of the child, e.g. intellectual skills would be more appropriate for a four-year-old child than for a five-month-old baby because it would not be so easy to collect information on the younger child.

Another example is physical development. This would be appropriate for a nine-month-old baby as there is plenty of physical development taking place, but not so suitable for a five-year-old child who has completed most stages of physical development.

It is more difficult to work on several areas of development, although it can be possible. It is usually more appropriate to focus on one area. You must choose carefully as the decisions you make now will affect the whole piece of work. Ask for advice if you need it to help you make the best choices. You need to be able to give clear reasons for the decisions you make.

Task title
Are the twins growing and developing as expected compared to each other and the development norms?

Suggest a range of suitable resources

It is important for you to list some possibilities about where you can look to find the information that you need, e.g. books, videos or DVDs, leaflets (see diagram below). You do not have to use all of them but you should consider all possible resources.

Consider the background information of the child/children

This is the research you carry out (using suitable sources) to find out information about the child you are going to be studying, e.g. age, likes and dislikes, skills that the child has acquired so far. The information you give should be specific to the age of the child. For example, the method of birth delivery and birth weight are not relevant to the intellectual development of a three-year-old child, but their ability to hold a pencil or crayon *is* an important factor.

Carrying out secondary research

It is important that you are aware of what a child in your chosen age range could be expected to be able to do. To find this out you should research a variety of sources to collect information. When you have collected the information, you need to select the parts that are most relevant and relate them to the child you are studying. You might want to create some charts or highlight specific important sections of information that you want to make use of.

It is important that you do not just copy lots of notes from textbooks or pages from the Internet as this is cheating (known as plagiarism). It is not helpful to you and it goes against copyright laws. It is also unacceptable to the examining body. Remember to reference any information you collect. Your research can be presented in any appropriate form, e.g. bullet points, spider diagrams, graphs, tables or charts. An example of how this can be done is given below.

Later in the task you will be able to use this information to help you to examine if the child is below average, average or above average in developmental progress for his or her age.

Development norms for my study child

The following information was gathered from my child development textbook. These are changes I should expect to see in my child, Megan, during the coming weeks:

Six months
- By six months babies are able to reach and grab things with both hands. They use their hands to touch and stroke things. They put most toys into their mouths.
- They enjoy imitating sounds and start babbling.
- They are usually wary of strangers although they find people quite fascinating.

Child study task: planning

SECTION 2: SELECTING AND PLANNING THE OBSERVATIONS

Possible ideas for the observations

When you have completed your research, you should understand more about what the child should be able to do. This should help you to find out and suggest a range of possible ideas and activities for the observations. You also need to think of ways of making this as interesting as possible for the child.

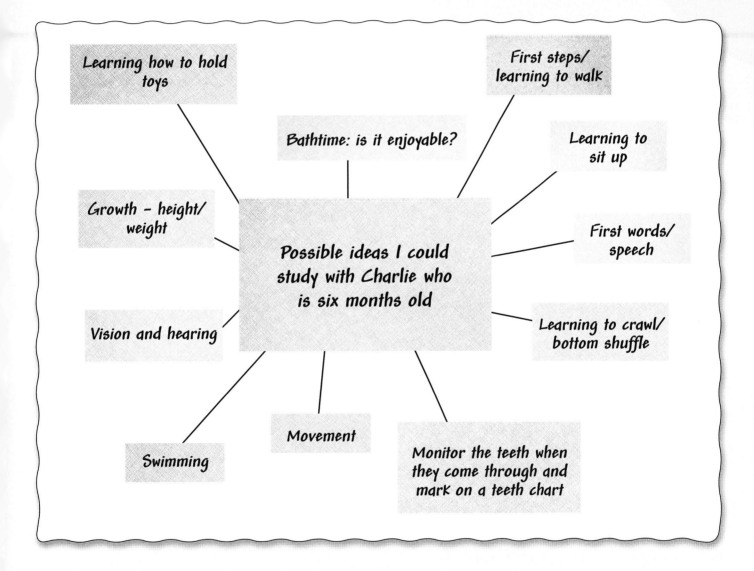

Variety of techniques

The observations you do should have lots of variety. They should be done using a range of methods such as longitudinal, naturalistic event sampling, etc.

Justifying choices

When you have decided what your observations will be, you need to give reasons for choosing them including why they are suitable for the child. Here is one way of doing this.

My choices of observations

Activity	Select/reject	Reason for choice/justification
Drawing	Reject	I have rejected this activity because Grace is too young to draw
Puzzles	Select	I have chosen this activity because Grace is starting to play with puzzles and I can observe how she grasps them
Activity cube	Select	I have chosen this so I can see how good Grace's hand-eye co-ordination is and if she understands what to do
Music and banging pots	Select	I want to see how Grace reacts and if her co-ordination is good enough to manage this. I also want to see if she likes the noise it makes
Building blocks	Select	This will be a good test of Grace's co-ordination and if she can balance things

Plans for observations

You need to plan what you intend to do for your observations, including how you will record what you observe.

Methods of recording results

To produce good-quality, interesting work it is a good idea to include many different ways of recording what you have observed. You could include an example of any recording charts in your planning, saying how and when they will be used.

The plans that you make should show clearly what you intend to do and you should be able to follow them to help you organise your work.

A table or chart is one way of doing this but there are many others that are suitable.

Child study task: observing and recording

SECTION 3: PRACTICAL OBSERVATIONS

Observations

The observations you have planned need to be carried out using a variety of methods and should show different ways of recording the activities in order for you to gain high marks.

Ideas can include bar charts and graphs. Examples of the child's work, such as a painting, drawing, collage, worksheet or sample of handwriting, would be ideal. Remember to stick to the things that you plan to do. Photographs that focus on what the child is doing, e.g. child looking down at his or her hands while playing a game, hands completing a jigsaw puzzle or doing a memory game, can be included as appropriate. These are a useful way of showing evidence of what the child can do. Your own written explanations or comments can accompany any pictures included.

Growth charts can also be used or copies of diagrams showing stages of development. The more interesting and wide-ranging your work is, the better your marks will be. Remember not to include full-face photographs in your work for reasons of child confidentiality.

Applying understanding to observations

The quality of explanation is particularly important here. You need to use the correct terminology to gain high marks.

It is important to show that you understand what you have observed. This can be done by explaining what you have seen happening during the observations and what you understand from doing the activity. Using the earlier research you collected will enable you to compare your study child to the development milestones or norms.

One way of comparing the child to what they should be doing is to create a table like the one above or a chart with the norms on it. These must be for the correct age range and show appropriate activities from the area of development being studied. There are many other ways that this can be done. You should choose those that you feel are most suited to

Sarah's improvement chart

This chart shows how Sarah's mobility skills have improved since my first visit.

	Visit 1	Visit 5
Roll on to tummy		
Lift head and chest, supporting themselves on their hands and arms	✓	✓
Use shoulders to pull themselves up into a sitting position	x	✓
Bear almost all of their own weight	✓	✓
Stand/sit with a straight back when held	✓	✓
Crawl or shuffle	✓	✓
Turn body to look sideways when stretching to reach an object	✓	✓
Stand holding on to furniture	x	✓

From this chart I can see that Sarah has developed well, maintaining her skills and improving in some areas. I would expect to see this type of improvement as Sarah has shown good muscle development and is starting to show more control, which is appropriate for her age and stage of development.

your style of work. Another example of a suitable way is to find quotes from textbooks and compare your child to these. If you choose to use quotes you must reference these appropriately.

When comparing the child to others, this can be done by observing the children playing together or by comparing the development norm charts for each of the children. You can design a chart with suitable headings to fit in with the information you have gained about your child and then compare the other child to your headings. Alternatively, you can write separately about each of the children, comparing what each one can do to the development norms you researched.

This section should include notes on how the child is progressing or has progressed during the time that you have been carrying out the work. You should look especially at the norms to see if they are behind the norms, at the norms or ahead of the expected norms for their age range. Remember they may be quicker with some things and a bit slower with others.

You should feel free to develop a style of your own to show the points you wish to make, as there is no particular way that this section must be done. What should be clear is that you understand what you have observed.

Child study task: conclusion and evaluation

SECTION 4: CONCLUSION AND EVALUATION

In this section you need to show a good level of understanding to achieve high marks. To review all aspects of the task you should look at the whole piece of work, stating what has been achieved in each section.

Explaining the things that you feel you have done well will help you to identify your strengths and you should say how you could improve on any weaker sections that are not quite so good.

Look back at the quality of your planning as this will have affected your results. Were you able to follow what you had planned to do?

Review your chosen task title and comment on how successful you have been in achieving what you set out to do. Draw logical conclusions about the work that you have completed, paying particular attention to the progress that the child has made since your work began.

Marks are awarded as part of this section for the overall quality of your written communication skills throughout the whole piece of work. This includes the use of correct terms/terminology or vocabulary along with the quality of your spelling and punctuation. Take care to read through your work and check it carefully.

An appropriate bibliography should be compiled, listing all of the book sources you have used in alphabetical order. This should be followed by a list of websites.

Written communication

The final area of the marking scheme in the evaluation is based on the level of the written communication in the task, which includes spelling, punctuation and grammar as well as the use of specialist terms/terminology. You should be aware at the start of the task that these factors will be assessed in the criteria. The evaluation is the area where continuous writing is likely to occur and where these marks are awarded (see below). However, the task as a whole will be looked at when awarding these marks.

Example of an evaluation report

I would have preferred to study a child who was a little older than Samir, perhaps about three years old, so that there could have been a wider choice of observations to choose from, but as I had no other child to observe I had to make do.

I am satisfied with my write-ups about the different developments and stages of progression because I feel that I have written short but concise notes.

I am pleased that I chose to study manipulative skills in particular because these linked closely with Samir's age and there were a lot of observations that I could plan that involved manipulative skills. With my task title I felt I didn't want to make it too specific because that would narrow down the types of activities for Samir, but by including the aspect of familiarity and favouritism it wasn't left too open-ended.

In the research and planning areas I made sure I researched well into the relevant stages of manipulative skills, as well as more general information on physical development.

I feel that I collected adequate information on Samir before I started to do my planning section. I made sure that when I was planning the activities for the observations Samir either had already done each of them so I knew he was capable or that he should be able to do them at his age.

Having seen Samir's capabilities I would perhaps have added an observation using beads and cotton reels for threading. I didn't include this initially because from my first few visits I didn't think he would be able to do this.

I produced a logical plan which I tried to follow but didn't manage:

o On Visit 1 I observed Samir with building blocks as I had planned and found out some important points as planned.

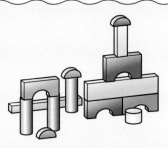

o Visit 2 was supposed to be a drawing activity but at the last minute I had to change the time of the visit. The new time suited Samir's bedtime rather than doing a drawing activity.

o Visit 3 was supposed to involve Duplo but in order to try and get on track with my plan I got Samir to do some drawing.

o Visit 4 was supposed to be garden activities but the weather wasn't appropriate. This observation was repeatedly postponed and eventually Samir's mother said she would prefer it if I didn't do this observation at all. Instead on this visit I got Samir to play again with the building blocks.

o Visit 7 was supposed to be modelling dough but when I arrived Samir was already playing with his Duplo and, as I hadn't already done the observation with Duplo, I decided that doing it on this occasion was best.

o I had planned for Visit 8 to be bedtime, but as I had already done this and not modelling dough I decided to do that instead.

I recorded my observations in a way which I felt was most appropriate for the types of observations I was carrying out. I didn't vary my methods of recording my evidence as much as I probably could have done. I did include a graph and a drawing but I felt that if I had used other methods, e.g. tick charts, I wouldn't have got as much information.

With Samir living only a few miles away it wasn't difficult for me to get to see him and his mother was very willing to co-operate. I was able to carry out all but one of my planned observations.

I found the write-ups of my visits difficult because I didn't want to repeat the information I'd already written in my task research. Also, the more observations I wrote up, the more I felt the content was becoming repetitive – this could be seen as a slight weakness in my work. I could have improved this by having a wider range of things to observe and by recording them with the use of more charts. Photographs would have also shown clearly what Samir was able to do. Overall, though, I felt my write-ups provided me with the information I'd set out to get, so they were successful from that point of view – that was one of my strengths.

I think the activities I planned allowed me to see the changes as Samir was progressing. I achieved this by planning a variety of activities.

I enjoyed the task analysis section, and writing about physical development in particular, because I prefer the theory side of this work. I had found and included only relevant information so I feel that this was a strength of my work.

I think I successfully interpreted my observations and I tried to relate this to my research into manipulative skills – again a strength. I managed to find a child to compare Samir with, which was good, but then found it difficult to observe much because Adam didn't know me and was obviously shy. This is a weakness in being able to apply my knowledge as I didn't have enough to say. I could have improved on this by including Adam on several occasions as that way he would have got more used to me. I could have then included the information on both of the boys and compared it to the development norms for this age group.

The importance of my work lies in the fact that I have showed an understanding of Samir's manipulative development and, therefore, I feel that this is an important factor in this piece of work.

My task title was 'How do the fine manipulative actions of an 18-month-old develop and differ according to the object they are playing with?' I have fulfilled my original intentions because I discovered that an 18-month-old can build a tower of nine blocks, do simple jigsaws and play with modelling dough. I can see this because the activities I chose to carry out in my observations were appropriate to the age and stage of the child's development, as well as being designed to give me the maximum information required in order for me to answer my task title well.

Short tasks

You need to submit three short tasks to complete this unit. Two of the short tasks will assess your skills in:

- planning
- practical work
- evaluation.

The third task will assess your investigative skills. Together, the three tasks make up 30 per cent of the total coursework marks – 60 marks in total (20 marks per task).

Each short task comprises the following sections:

- planning
- carrying out
- evaluation.

You need to complete each section in detail to produce a good-quality piece of work. Each of the three tasks should demonstrate different skills and knowledge.

PLANNING

You need to produce a plan that explains clearly what you intend to do in order to complete the task. Look carefully at the task you have been given and identify what you have got to do to complete the work.

Produce a task outline or introduction to explain what you intend to do for the whole task, making it clear which type of task it is (practical or investigation).

In order to carry out the task, you need to work out which resources you are going to need or use. If you are doing an investigation, think carefully about which investigative techniques or skills you want to include or use, depending on what it is you are trying to find out. There are lots of things you could do in an investigation, such as:

- surveys
- questionnaires
- comparisons
- interviews
- visits.

It is a good idea to do a range of different things to find out the necessary information. This will allow you to produce an interesting piece of work. You should select a range of resources that could be suitable and then decide which of these are the most suitable for this particular task. When you have chosen the ones you want to use, create a plan stating what you are intending to do. You can do this in any way that you like, but possible suggestions include:

- write out an order of work, similar to a method, explaining each point
- create a flow chart showing the sequence of what you will be doing and the order in which you will do it
- give an explanation of each of your chosen resources and how you will use them in this task
- suggest various techniques that are suitable for the topic, explaining how you will use them.

Whichever method you decide to use, your plan must show exactly which activities you are intending to carry out in order to complete the overall task. You can use all or a combination of the above suggestions to make sure that you plan thoroughly before you start to carry out the work.

The planning section provides your opportunity to explain what you intend to do to carry out the task.

If necessary, any appropriate research should not be in planning, but could be incorporated into the carrying out section. However, only include it if it is really needed. Researching does not mean copying lots of notes from your sources.

CARRYING OUT

There are two parts to carrying out this work:

- organisation
- outcome.

Organisation

The organisation section of the practical task is where you are marked on doing the work to make something, such as:

- a leaflet to provide information
- a game to develop a particular skill, e.g. counting

- a book to provide activities, textures, for interest or entertainment
- a dish for a child's packed lunch
- a snack or meal
- a mobile to hang above a cot.

In the investigation, you could:

- conduct a survey
- produce a questionnaire
- carry out an interview
- do a visit
- complete a comparative study.

Whatever it is you are doing, you need to:

- work accurately
- use a variety of skills or techniques
- produce work of a high standard that you can be proud of
- include a written description of what you have done.

Outcome

The outcome that you have produced must be of high quality to achieve good marks. There should be evidence of something you have made, such as a photograph of the mobile or of the game being played. The results of any investigative work should be presented appropriately using a range of suitable techniques to show the information clearly, such as tally charts, graphs, bar charts, pie charts and photographs.

EVALUATION

When evaluating your work, explain the strengths that you have shown throughout the task. Any weaker areas should be identified with suggestions on how they can be improved on. Any items that you have produced can be trialled on a child to see if they are successful and you can include any appropriate comments or conclusions.

The success of your work depends on how well you have managed to carry out the task. You should describe how well you have worked and, if you have carried out everything that you planned to do, give examples wherever possible. Conclude the piece of work by ensuring that you refer back to the task title, explaining what you have managed to achieve.

Note: key terms are in **bold**